EXECUTION

TOOLS & TECHNIQUES

EXECUTION

TOOLS & TECHNIQUES

Bart Rommel

Loompanics Unlimited
Port Townsend, Washington

EXECUTION: TOOLS AND TECHNIQUES

Printed in USA

Published by:
Loompanics Unlimited
PO Box 1197
Port Townsend, WA 98368
Loompanics Unlimited is a division of Loompanics Enterprises, Inc.

ISBN 1-55950-051-4
Library of Congress Catalog Card Number 90-63309

Cover Photo: "Waiting," 1908, Library of Congress Photograph
#LC-US262-14621

Contents

1. Introduction 1
2. The Power of the State 5
3. History of Execution 9
4. Execution in Popular Culture 19
5. Execution Customs..27
6. Hanging 37
7. Beheading 43
8. Execution Horrors 49
9. Shooting 55
10. Execution by Gas 67
11. Electrocution 73

12. Lethal Injection 87
13. Ceremonial Self-Execution 99
14. The Future of Executions............................103
Index...115

1

Introduction

Killing has been a part of history for as long as there has been history. When an individual kills, it's murder. When the state kills, it's execution.

Execution is ceremonial killing, done by the power of and under the auspices of the state. Execution is one of man's oldest customs, and there are documented instances of execution for various reasons going back at least as far as the ancient Greeks. No doubt, there were executions before, but these occurred before written history.

People have been sentenced to death for many reasons, some of which appear frivolous today. Ancient states executed people for heresy, as did officials of various religions. In Roxbury, Massachusetts, a teenage boy named Thomas Graunger was hanged for having sex with animals.

Motives for executions have varied; so have methods. Some techniques were picturesque and bizarre. Drawing and quartering was one of the more spectacular techniques devised many centuries ago. Other methods were simple, effective, and economical, such as the shot to the back of the head. In the United States, high tech execution reached its peak with the electric chair and the gas chamber.

One of the darker aspects of human history is that the technology of death has always been far ahead of the technology of preserving life. During the 18th and 19th Centuries, there were hangmen noted for their skill, and the guillotine was the apex of death technology. At the same time, doctors were little more than faith healers, and medical technology was so simple that it scarcely existed.

There have been several themes running through the history and techniques of execution. First is the right of the state to put to death various persons whom it deems deserve it. Another is the persistent debate regarding the purpose and validity of capital punishment. Yet another is the theme of retribution. Finally, we have a trend towards making executions tidy, humane, and even painless. Centuries ago, execution methods were especially harsh and cruel. Today, most executions throughout the world are brief, with emphasis on finishing as soon as possible.

Execution methods tend to reflect the country's culture and economic status. At the lowest level, the People's Republic of China uses a pistol shot to the back of the head, appropriate for a country with a very low standard of living. The most outlandish methods of execution are in the United States, the planet's wealthiest country. It's very expensive to build a gas chamber or electric chair for the ceremonial killing of offenders, but the United States can afford it.

This book will survey the history, motives, and techniques of execution. We'll cover ancient techniques, study the development of the concept of execution, and describe some of the more bizarre methods.

The emphasis will be on the technology of death, with little on the philosophy. Execution is bizarre, cruel, and nasty, and anyone who thinks otherwise is ignoring the obvious facts. State killing is for people who commit bizarre, nasty, and cruel crimes, not for jaywalkers and shoplifters. Still, many well-meaning people feel that execution is unjustified, and terribly uncivilized. We also find, for example, that opponents of capital punishment express a lot of concern over the rights of the criminal, but practically ignore the victim's rights. We'll look very quickly at some of the social issues surrounding execution. However, because most of the philosophizing is mere intellectual masturbation, it's not worth taking up much space, and our main effort will be the study of death technology.

2

The Power of the State

Ever since people first banded together to form tribes, there have been methods of enforcing both public order and the will of the majority. A system of rewards was for those who showed outstanding accomplishments. Various punishments awaited those who went against the rules or mores.

During most of human history, punishments consisted of fines, corporal punishment, banishment, mutilation, and death. The concept of prolonged confinement was almost unknown, because the development of the penitentiary did not come until the 18th Century, in America.

The simplest, least expensive, and most permanent method of enforcing the power of the state was by killing the guilty. We see that from the very start, the state took to itself the power of life and death over its citizens. It has never mattered how advanced or humane the regime. Death was always the ultimate sanction. Even the ancient Athenians, who were perhaps the most "civilized" of ancient cultures, killed their own citizens.

The basic principle is that the state has the right to kill for its own purposes. This comes from custom, written law, and religious traditions and teachings. Today, some people quote from the Bible to justify capital punishment. Other religions have laid out very specific punishments. The Koran specifies that a thief shall have his hands cut off. This still occurs in various Moslem states in the Middle East. Beheading is a punishment awaiting transgressors in Saudi Arabia.

The legal mechanism for state killing has varied, but always had the trappings of legal procedure. In ancient times, a hearing of sorts, before a committee of citizens or administrators, was the form. Anglo-Saxon tradition developed the idea of a trial by a jury of peers. Further development of the legal system resulted in a very formal, multi-stage system of arraignment, trial, and appeals, before an execution could take place.

An important expression of the power of the state is putting to death those who seek to overthrow it, or harm it in any way. Treason has always been one of the most serious crimes anyone could commit, and today death is still the punishment for treason. In countries such as Switzerland, which have abolished capital punishment for civil crimes, death by firing squad is still possible for traitors tried under military law. Other Western countries which still keep the death penalty for certain wartime crimes are Denmark, France, Italy, Holland, Norway, and Spain.[1]

We'll see, by studying the history of executions, that the power of the state has always been the main ingredient, although applied in different ways and for different purposes. In ancient times, despots executed people who threatened their power. The state and church combined to kill the unfaithful in medieval times. In modern times, the state sees to the welfare of the people, and capital punishment is for murderers and other serious criminals. However, we still have despotic regimes that use the power of the state for their own ends.

Sources

1. *Capital Punishment and the American Agenda*, Franklin E. Zimring and Gordon Hawkins, New York, Cambridge University Press, 1986, p. 5.

3

History of Execution

Classic Executions

Perhaps the most famous execution of ancient times was that of Socrates, forced to drink a cup of hemlock because he was an intellectual non-conformist and allegedly corrupted Greek youth. By Greek standards of the era, his practicing homosexuality was not objectionable, but his spreading of radical ideas was. In one sense, Socrates got unusual consideration, because conventional methods of execution in ancient Greece were burning at the stake and crucifixion.[1]

The Bible

There are references to executions in the Bible. Harlots and adulteresses were stoned to death, for example, but the dating of these events is open to question. There is mention of inflicting death on disrespectful or disobedient sons, and on women who were not virgins on their wedding nights.[2] Sex with animals was also indication for death, for both the human perpetrator and the animal involved.

The most noted execution in the Bible is the crucifixion of Jesus Christ, who like Socrates, was sentenced to death for preaching radical ideas. At the time, according to the Biblical account, property theft was also cause for capital punishment, and Christ was placed between two thieves at his death. A difference between the executions was that several nails held Christ to the cross, while ropes served for the others. Another difference was that executioners placed especially hideous criminals upside-down on the cross, which was definitely more merciful because blood rushing to their brains rendered them unconscious quickly, sparing them suffering.

Another variant on crucifixion was that passersby or soldiers would sometimes break the prisoner's bones while he was hanging. Other measures were to beat or whip him. Blows with a scourge would tear the flesh open, sometimes even disemboweling him on the spot.

Medieval Executions

In medieval times, certain strange methods of inflicting death came into use. At that time, the emphasis appeared to be on protracted suffering, and spectacular results, not efficient killing. Burning became popular as a way of executing witches, heretics, and other persons offensive to monarchs or religious authorities. English troops burned Joan of Arc at the stake on May 30, 1431. Drawing and quartering, with a draft animal attached to each limb, was another spectacular way to execute the condemned.

Disemboweling was another method, often combined with hanging or drawing and quartering. This saw use as late as 1812.[3]

The tools of the Spanish Inquisition are worth noting, more for their bizarre aspect than their efficiency. The rack was a device consisting of a platform and a windlass. The platform was long enough to hold a person stretched out with arms extended over the head. Ropes held the feet to one end of the rack, while the executioner attached the wrists to the windlass. Turning the windlass tightened the ropes, and stretched the entire body. The spine would eventually break apart, causing death.

The Iron Maiden was another tool for death by torture. This coffin-like device had spikes on the inside. Closing a person into the Iron Maiden would both confine him and drive the spikes part-way into his body.

The "auto-da-fe," or act of faith, was execution by ceremonial burning at the stake. This was the final act of repentance forced upon the unfaithful by Spanish zealots.

Another method of causing death was "ducking," or drowning. In this method, the subject was tied to a long pole, which the execution crew would pivot into a lake, ducking the individual for increasing periods, until death came by drowning. In some cases, the intent was to persuade the subject to confess, after which the execution would proceed as scheduled. Eleven Gypsy women suffered this fate in Edinburgh in 1623.[4]

In earlier times, execution of children was accepted. Pre-teens were subject to execution for petty thefts as late as 1808, in England.[5]

Recent Efforts at Abolition

There has been a death penalty abolition movement in the United States for well over a century, as there has been in Europe. Many states have tried to abandon capital punishment, but recently, with the increase in violent crime, the pendulum has been swinging the other way.

There are many reasons and justifications given for retaining capital punishment.

Punishment and Retribution

There have been many motives for capital punishment. Punishment and retribution were early justifications for execution. The authority for punishment came both from the power of the state and from religion. Execution, in such cases, served a divine purpose.

Retribution as justification for capital punishment is becoming respectable once more. For centuries, opponents of capital punishment took the position that execution is unworthy of civilized society. Perhaps it is. However, in the modern era, some people are honest enough to admit that we aren't necessarily civilized, but merely organized, and that mistaking one for the other leads to serious problems.

Victims of crime, including relatives and survivors, often experience psychological damage, such as depression. This becomes worse if the perpetrator obviously gets away with it. Confidence in the rule of law, and in the power of the state, suffers if criminals go unpunished. One way to cope with this is to see to it that perpetrators of particularly vicious crimes suffer execution.

Salvation

The Inquisition brought another reason for execution: to save the person's soul. Death by torture was, in this theological view, preferable to life outside of the correct faith.

Deterrence

This is a relatively modern view, an outgrowth of the decline of religion. Previously, people were good or evil, and their conduct depended on their goodness or sinfulness. Today, there are those who advocate that punishment of the guilty serves as an example to others contemplating crime.

In two instances, deterrence undeniably works. The threat of execution is a mental hazard to spies looking forward to operating in enemy territory. The person executed is also "deterred" from committing any more crimes. A better term is "incapacitated." As we shall see, there is statistical evidence that capital punishment affects the murder rate.

Countries with high crime rates have not reduced them by imposing capital punishment. Banning capital punishment has not resulted in clear-cut increases in crime, as many other factors affect the picture.

Humanizing Death

A theme running through executions as retribution was "an eye for an eye and a tooth for a tooth." The idea was that the condemned criminal should suffer in the same way as his victim.

In cases where the victim was impersonal, or the death penalty was for heresy or non-conformism, some rulers felt nevertheless that the execution should be as painful as possible. Some methods of execution seemed to be specially designed to inflict pain and provide a long and drawn-out death. One of England's kings was executed by red-hot irons inserted into the rectum. Burning at the stake was another exceptionally painful way to die.

In more modern times, there's been a move away from cruelty, and during this century the pendulum has swung towards the other extreme. In Western countries that still have capital punishment, the main concern seems to be to provide a death as painless as possible. In certain ways, this seems absurd, because today the only civil crime punishable by death is murder, and some murderers have killed their victims in particularly cruel and ferocious ways. Concern over making the condemned murderer's manner of dying humane and pain-free is typical of "bleeding heart" thinking, which concerns itself unduly with the rights of the criminal while totally neglecting the rights of the victim.

However, there is a practical reason for painless executions: public relations. Twelve jurors are more likely to convict if they have the assurance that the guilty party won't be tortured. Despite the seriousness of the crime of murder, and the cruel ways in which some killers treat their victims, there are still squeamish people serving on juries, and defense attorneys carefully study jury panels to include at least one on their jury, if possible.

In the United States today, executions are in transition. The 1972 Supreme Court decision that struck down capital punishment laws as then written proclaimed that they were arbitrary and capricious. Various states hurried to re-write their capital punishment laws, and on July 1, 1976, the Supreme Court ruled that capital punishment, by itself, is not cruel or unusual, but also struck down laws prescribing mandatory capital punishment for murder. The result was that there must be a reason for the death sentence, usually that the crime was committed in a specially brutal or heinous manner. Once the road was clear to capital punishment, Gary Gilmore became the first to die under the new rules, a Utah firing squad ending his life on January 17, 1977.

As of the end of 1988, two states, Utah and Idaho, prescribed death by firing squad. Both also allow lethal injection. Other states with the death penalty are as follows:

Hanging: Delaware, Montana, New Hampshire, and Washington.

Gas: Arizona, California, Colorado, Maryland, and North Carolina.

Electrocution: Alabama, Connecticut, Florida, Georgia, Indiana, Kentucky, Louisiana, Nebraska, Ohio, Pennsylvania, South Carolina, Tennessee, and Virginia.

Lethal Injection: Arkansas, Idaho, Illinois, Mississippi, Missouri, Montana, Nevada, New Jersey, New Mexico, North Carolina, Oklahoma, Oregon, South Dakota, Texas, Utah, Washington, and Wyoming.

As we can see from the above lists, a few states in addition to Utah and Idaho provide for alternate methods of execution. Montana and Washington have both hanging and lethal injection. North Carolina has either gas or injection.[6]

A few states have no death penalty. These are: Alaska, Iowa, Kansas, Michigan, Minnesota, Maine, Massachusetts, New

York, North Dakota, Rhode Island, Vermont, West Virginia, and Wisconsin. The District of Columbia also has no death penalty.[7]

It's interesting to note the different mores in various parts of the country, reflected in whether or not states have the death penalty. Only one Southern state, West Virginia, lacks capital punishment. Most states without it are concentrated in the Northeast and Midwest. In some cases, abolition is associated with a particularly outspoken person, such as New York's Governor Mario Cuomo, who is a notable opponent of capital punishment.

At one time, capital punishment appeared to be associated with states which had high crime rates, and whose legislatures were willing to use drastic measures for coping with crime. Today, paradoxically, some areas with very high murder rates have no death penalty. Both New York State and the District of Columbia, with crime and murder rates among the very highest in the country, lack a capital punishment law. Detroit also has a very high crime rate, but Michigan does not have the death penalty.

Let's now examine the roles executions play in popular culture. We'll see how legalized killings work in both fact and fiction.

Sources

1. *Executions*, George V. Bishop, Los Angeles, CA, Sherbourne Press, 1965, p. 36.

2. *Crime and Capital Punishment*, Robert H. Loeb, Jr., in consultation with Professor George F. Cole, New York, Impact Books, 1986, p. 18.

3. *Ibid.*, p. 21.

4. *Ibid.*, p. 23.

5. *Ibid.*, p. 24.

6. *1989 Information Please Almanac*, p. 801.

7. *1990 World Almanac*, p. 850.

4

Execution in Popular Culture

The mass media presents strange views of executions. One reason is sensationalism, purposeful distortions to increase the size of the audience. Another reason is media manipulation by advocates of one stance or another. This extends even to scholarly works.

Advocacy

An example is in the preface to a serious study of capital punishment, in which the authors express a very cavalier view of victims' rights.[1] In this context, it's not surprising, because these authors seem to feel that abolition of the death penalty is, or should be, trendy.[2] They also express disappointment that executions resumed in the United States, despite the view of the majority that capital punishment is legitimate.

There have been several public opinion polls to show that, in recent years, capital punishment has been the majority view. However, we find evidence of an elitist attitude in writers opposed to capital punishment. Robert Loeb, while acknowledging that Gallup Polls in 1981 and 1985 showed that an overwhelming majority of Americans support the death penalty, dismisses these results with the remark that Americans are uninformed.[3]

It's even fashionable to be concerned over the convicted killer's pain and suffering, while ignoring that of the victim.[4] We read gory descriptions of executions, but seldom similarly detailed accounts of what the condemned did to earn this penalty. This is the sort of thinking that has set back law enforcement in this and other countries.

Poverty and ignorance, as well as brutal parents, bad companions, and the other classic causes of crime, have always existed. Crime rates have risen and fallen, according to measures governments took to control them. During the second half of the Twentieth Century, executions fell in the United States, while the murder rate rose. In 1957, for example, there were 65 executions in the entire country, and 8,060 murders. By 1965, executions had fallen to seven for the entire year, but murders were up to 9,850. In 1968, there were no executions at all, and there were 13,650 murders. Those who argue against the death penalty maintain that the rise in population accounted for most of this increase.

No executions took place at all until 1977, when one killer, Gary Gilmore, was executed, and the number of murders had risen to 19,560. There were two executions in 1979, and one in 1981, by which time the numbers of murders per year had risen to 22,520.[5] Although other factors also affect the murder rate, it's pretty clear from these figures which way the trend is going.

By March, 1985, there had been 41 executions in the United States. There were 18 executions in 1985 and 18 in 1986. There were 25 in 1987, and 11 in 1988. Edward R. Byrne, electrocuted in the state prison at Angola, Louisiana, on June 14, 1988, became the 100th person to die since executions resumed. One hundred twelve prisoners had been executed by June 19, 1989. By 1987, the number of murders had dropped to 20,096, according to FBI figures, while the population of the United States had continued to increase. Despite the protestations of the "bleeding hearts," it's crystal-clear that when executions go down, murders rise, and when executions go up, murders go down.

Still, we find that people against the death penalty advocate the most preposterous beliefs. One is Eugene B. Block, who stated, without citing any proof, that the three men in Georgia who hate their jobs the most are those who have to pull the switches on the panel controlling the electric chair.[6] He puts forth this view without mentioning the identities of these men, or quoting from any of their statements. He cites no figures for turn-over rates among executioners from any state.

It's hard to accept that, in a country of 240 million people, the majority of whom favor capital punishment, there is a shortage of people with the courage of their convictions. Anyone who advocates capital punishment should find it easy, if he has the courage of his convictions, to moonlight several evenings a year to earn extra dollars.

With technology advancing methods of inflicting death, executions are no longer exclusively men's work. It takes a strong arm to wield an axe, but only a hand to pull a switch or push the plunger on a syringe. With sexism on the way out, female executioners may be on their way into common acceptance.

Fictional Executions

Novels about totalitarian systems often contain executions of people who have fallen into disfavor with the regime. Arthur Koestler's novel, *Darkness at Noon*, is a fictional account of the Moscow trials of the late 1930s. In it, the central character meets his death after protracted interrogation, during which he had confessed. The executioner walks him down a hallway, and shoots him in the back of the head with a small pistol he had kept concealed up his sleeve.

The theme recurs in George Orwell's novel, *1984*. Winston Smith, the central character, goes through a painful interrogation and "brainwashing," knowing that sooner or later, an executioner will walk him down a corridor. The theme is that the execution is always without warning, a bullet in the back of the head.

Crime novels sometimes contain execution scenes, which may or may not be realistic. Roderick Thorpe's novel, *The Detective*, has a scene in which the hero attends the electrocution of a suspect whom he had arrested. The motion picture based upon that novel, with Frank Sinatra playing the role of the detective, shows the death chamber scene graphically.

One of the most extraordinary fictional books dealing with this topic was written by the son of a former prison official. *Deathwork*, by James McLendon, New York, Lippincott, 1977, is a novel based on the resumption of executions in Florida. In this novel, the governor of Florida is a death penalty advocate who has scheduled four condemned criminals to die on the same day. The explicit and detailed descriptions of the electric chair, and the executions of the four subjects, is unique in literature.

From this book, we learn the construction details of the electrodes attached to the prisoner: a cap and an ankle piece. We also learn that the electrode in the cap has a natural sponge soaked in salt water to help conductivity. Prisoners wear special diapers, to soak up urine involuntarily released when the high-voltage current hits. Florida's death machine is a special generator that produces 2,250 volts for 5 seconds, then drops to 1,000 volts for 25 seconds, through four cycles.

The descriptions of the effects of electrocution on the four condemned prisoners are meticulously detailed. We read how the electric pulses cause fibrillation of the heart in one prisoner, and how another bites his tongue during his convulsions, while his finger joints snap at the shock. The second prisoner doesn't die with the first application of the current, which has dried out the sponge. The second jolt begins to burn the skin on his head, and smoke rises from under the cap.

Motion Pictures

The execution theme has been prominent in many motion pictures, especially the gangster films of the thirties and forties. James Cagney, Barton MacLane, and other movie tough guys walked the last mile on the screen. During that era, scripts stressed that these gangsters were getting what they deserved, for crime does not pay.

Decades later, there would be another theme in motion pictures, for the abolitionists had written some scripts and gotten them produced. One of the early films, *I Want To Live*, purportedly a quasi-documentary, starred Susan Hayward as Barbara Graham. The theme of the film was that Graham was really innocent, but suffered execution by gas because of California's brutal and insensitive criminal justice system. This was so successful at the box office that, years later, there was a remake starring Lindsay Wagner.

If Hollywood could rehabilitate Barbara Graham, why not Caryl Chessman? Although Chessman had been nothing but a petty thug before his death sentence, the screen character was played by the charismatic and sympathetic Alan Alda. Without knowing the facts of the real case, it's hard to believe that Alan Alda deserved to sit in the gas chamber and inhale cyanide gas, as he was shown to do in the movie. By the time this film appeared, censorship standards had faded away, and explicitness was the order of the day. The film shows Alan Alda walking with quiet dignity into the execution chamber. Guards strap him into a metal chair in the "green room," and one of them advises him to breathe deeply when the gas comes, to make it easier. At a nod from the warden, the executioner releases the pellets into the acid. Alda goes into convulsions, while the telephone rings and the warden answers. A last-minute stay of execution came a minute too late, ending the film on a good dramatic note.

Now that we've seen how the popular media treats capital punishment, let's proceed to the way executions are in real life. There have arisen a number of customs and conventions surrounding executions, some of which persist even today. We'll examine these next.

Sources

1. *Capital Punishment and the American Agenda*, Franklin E. Zimring and Gordon Hawkins, New York, Cambridge University Press, 1986, p. xvi.

2. *Ibid.*, pp. 3-6.
3. *Crime and Capital Punishment*, Robert H. Loeb, Jr., in consultation with Professor George F. Cole, New York, Impact Books, 1986, p. 13.
4. *Capital Punishment and the American Agenda*, p. 112.
5. *Capital Punishment*, Edited by Thomas Draper, New York, The H. W. Wilson Company, 1985, p. 123.
6. *When Men Play God: The Fallacy of Capital Punishment*, Eugene B. Block, San Francisco, CA, Cragmont Publications, 1983, pp. 88-89.

5

Execution Customs

An array of customs has grown around executions. Some have developed through tradition, and are now prescribed by law or regulations. Others are still informal, and vary with time and place.

The Death Warrant

In individual executions, there is usually a piece of paper to satisfy the demands of orderly bureaucracy. This may be a court order, or an order signed by a state governor, military judge, or commander. Whatever the form, it legalizes the execution, and presumably absolves those involved from personal responsibility. With a written order, they are acting under the law.

The Death Watch

A special guard usually stands over the prisoner during his last hours or days, to prevent him from taking his own life. If the judgment of the court or other authority is that he be put to death by the means prescribed by law, so must it be. Committing suicide would be cheating the state, and is forbidden. Therefore, during the last days or hours, the condemned person is in a special cell, with eyes upon him every moment.

If a prisoner succeeds in taking his own life, a scandal inevitably follows. When Hermann Goering, Nazi Germany's Number Two man after the Fuehrer, took a cyanide pill a few hours before he was to be hanged, it was a headline story. The prison commander, Colonel Andrus, lost his post, and his career was blemished.

Witnesses

By law, in many countries and states, there's a prescribed number of witnesses to the execution. Some required witnesses are the prison warden or his assistant, and various officials. Sometimes, the victim's survivors are allowed to witness the execution of a murderer.

In some countries, executions are public events, even being televised. Perhaps there's a belief that viewing the execution serves as a deterrent to crime. Executions used to be public in the United States and Britain during the Nineteenth Century, but authorities discovered that public hangings often gave pickpockets excellent opportunities for plying their trade.

In the United States and all territories it controls, executions are restricted affairs. They always take place in secluded areas, with the general public and the media excluded. Witnesses may not bring cameras, and any photographs taken must be for official purposes only. This is a general rule in Western countries.

The Last Meal

Popular culture has it that a condemned person may order anything he wishes for his last meal. This is largely untrue. In most countries, the last meal is nothing special, and in fact there may not even be a last meal. In the United States, prison wardens may allow the condemned the choice of whatever's available, but obviously there are some foods that are simply out of the question.

The Last Cigarette

This is a very strong tradition in military executions, but often honored in the breach. The U. S. Army's regulations governing execution make no mention of a last cigarette at the site of execution. If the condemned smokes, he'll most likely have to smoke his last cigarette before the ceremony begins.

A joke that made the rounds a couple of decades ago concerned the prisoner who refused a last cigarette: "No, thanks. Those things are bad for your health!" he said.

The Last Drink

Tradition and expediency hold that the prisoner should have a drink of alcohol if he wishes, to help him through his final hours or minutes. The last drink came about less through compassion than through the need to expedite the proceedings. An execution can be very messy if the prisoner struggles, because someone fighting for his life will resist with desperate fury. It will take many strong men to drag him to the execution chamber, or tie him to a post, or hold him still long enough to place the noose around his neck. A few drinks can stifle the prisoner's anxiety and make him easier to handle. It may even be necessary to have the prisoner intoxicated to make him more tractable.

Religious Counsel

Another tradition is to have a clergyman present to counsel the condemned during his final hours. In Catholic countries, this is very strong tradition, as that faith teaches that everyone should repent his sins before death, and to allow a person to go to his death without confession is itself a grave sin.

In most other countries, having clergy of his faith present is permissible, if the condemned so wishes. The clergyman may remain with the condemned during his final minutes or hours, and even during the execution.

Last Letters

Often, condemned prisoners are allowed to write one or more last letters to friends and relatives. In the American military, regulations specify that letters are subject to censorship.

Last Visitors

When practical, officials allow condemned persons to have final visits with family and/or friends. Regulations vary, and there may be a limit on time or number.

Last Words

Often, the condemned person has the opportunity to make a last statement, to the warden of the prison, the officer in charge of the execution detail, or to the witnesses in general. This is required by U. S. Army execution regulations, for example, and is a custom followed in many places.

The Last Mile

Traditionally, the condemned walks to his place of death. "The last mile" is a colloquialism, and the journey is never that long. In the interests of speed, the prisoner usually has to walk only a few yards. If the place of execution is in a remote location, there's always a means of transport to take him there as quickly as possible.

Sometimes, condemned felons can't even manage to walk the last few yards, and guards have to carry or drag them. The usual interpretation of this is that the prisoner suffered a loss of courage or moral fiber at the last moment. At times, as we shall see, there's another explanation.

The escort detail takes the prisoner from his cell or holding area, and walks him to the place of execution. This can be very difficult if the prisoner resists. Some escort details, as in the armed forces, carry rifles or pistols, but in civilian prisons, the rule is: "No guns inside the walls." They have to control the prisoner with pinch-clamps, handcuffs, or a belly band with wrist straps.

Extracting a resisting prisoner from his cell can be very difficult. This is when the detail needs a way to incapacitate the condemned person, and make him docile enough to lead to the execution chamber. The best way is CAP-STUN II, which is an aerosol subject restraint. This causes involuntary closing of the eyes, coughing, and loss of muscle control. It's not necessary to be inside the cell to use it, or to be in close contact with the prisoner, as with electronic "stun guns." Spraying the prisoner's face from outside the bars causes immediate collapse, and the aerosol dissipates quickly enough not to be a nuisance to the guards.

The Blindfold

Another tradition is that the condemned is spared the sight of rifles leveled at him, or the sight of the noose or electric chair. Much of this is myth. In reality, a black hood is often used to spare witnesses the sight of the condemned person's facial contortions at the moment of death. During electrocution, the prisoner often bites his tongue.

A persistent story is that of the condemned military man who refuses a blindfold. One account of this happening is questionable. Another persistent myth is the condemned requesting, and being granted, the right to issue orders to the firing squad. This is legend, and no documented case exists of this bravado.

Medical Services

Some doctors, including members of the American Medical Association, have stated that doctors are sworn to save life, not to take it, and that no ethical doctor would participate in the death process. This is typical hypocrisy. History shows that doctors have often taken part in executions. The guillotine, for example, was the invention of a doctor. A doctor locates the subject's heart with a stethoscope and places a paper target over it as an aiming point for the firing squad.

Except for hurried executions, a doctor is present, both to attend to the prisoner's last needs and to certify death. It may be expedient to administer a sedative to calm the prisoner and make him easier to handle. In extreme cases, it may be desirable to have the prisoner in a stupor to avoid a struggle.

In military and civilian executions, there's often a legal requirement of formal certification of death. Only a doctor can provide this.

The Coup de Grace

"Coup de grace" is a French phrase that means "mercy shot," and is a feature of death by firing squad. The need for the coup de grace arose from the uncertainty of quick death by shooting, and the poor marksmanship of some firing squad members. In theory, a volley of bullets to the heart should kill quickly, but in practice the condemned person often lingers. This may be because destroying the heart does not cause instant death, and often not even loss of consciousness. It also happens that all bullets may miss the heart, striking elsewhere on the body. To end the condemned's suffering, an officer or sergeant fires a pistol shot into his head immediately after the main volley.

Claiming the Body

It's customary for relatives to claim the body after execution. If nobody claims the body, disposal is by cheapest way, either burial in "potter's field," or by cremation.

Secrecy

Before the Twentieth Century, executions were often public spectacles, both for deterrence and to satisfy the crowd that justice had been done. In only a few instances during this century have executions been public. One spectacular example was the rash of quick court-martials that took place at the sports stadium in Havana shortly after Castro's troops overran the city. Members of Batista's regime, especially his secret police, got short trials and fast executions by firing squad.

Executioners used to be public figures, even celebrities, and in some instances the trade passed from father to son. The Sanson family provided Parisian executioners from 1688 to 1847, for example. A celebrated English hangman was William Calcraft, who practiced during the middle of the last century. Today, executioners are usually anonymous.

In most Western countries, executions take place in seclusion, although a public announcement accompanies them. At times, members of the press may be witnesses.

In some countries, executions have not only been removed from public view, but have been classified operations. German mobile execution squads, for example, were not publicized to the German people during World War II. In Soviet Russia, there have been many "show trials," but also an indeterminate number of "administrative" trials, followed by secret executions.

Secret arrests and executions in recent times have gotten quasi-official recognition. The term, "Argentine Method," comes from the era of military regime in Argentina.[1] This was known as the "dirty war," during which death squads of police and military officers kidnapped opponents of the regime and executed them without public trial.

Now that we've examined the customs and circumstances surrounding executions, let's move on to the nuts and bolts of various methods. The first we'll consider is hanging.

Sources

1. *New Words*, LeMay, Lerner, and Taylor, New York, Facts on File, 1988, p. 6.

6

Hanging

Hanging is a low-tech way of putting to death, and was a favorite method of execution in the United States until well into the 20th Century. It became so much a part of American culture that it was a preferred method of vigilantes, and even became corrupted in American English. Proper English uses the past tense "hanged" to denote execution at the end of a rope. Some people mistakenly use the word "hung," which actually applies to a painting or other inanimate object.

Hanging took hold in England several centuries ago, and the method endured until modern times, remaining the official method of civil execution until Parliament abolished capital punishment during the 1960s. One of the early celebrities among English hangmen was Jack Ketch, whose career spanned the years between 1663 and 1686.[1] Ketch was actually a prolific professional executioner who also handled the beheadings, which were fading out at the time.

Executions have always been a messy business, and much of the modern effort has gone to making them more tidy. In Elizabethan England and the years after, beheading was so poorly regarded that condemned people would, if they could afford it, pay a tip to their executioners not to botch the job and cause them prolonged suffering. One sad case was that of Lord Russell, sentenced to death in 1683. He knew that the standard operating procedure at the time was for the condemned man to kneel and for the executioner to chop off his head freehand, relying on skill and luck to do the job tidily. Lord Russell accordingly arranged for Jack Ketch to get a large payment in advance for doing a quick and neat job.

Ketch apparently had a drinking problem, and spent the evening before the execution either celebrating his good fortune or forgetting his past in high-octane drinking. The result was that his aim was unsure the next morning, and he botched the job, finally having to cut the Lord's head off with a knife. This was one of the incidents which led to more scientific methods of inducing quick death.

The Technology of Hanging

Hanging developed tangentially from garroting and strangulation, ancient but slow methods. In England, it first was an official method of execution in 1334, during the reign of Edward III.[2] At the time, death by hanging was merely slow strangulation. Being "strung up" at the end of a rope was unpleasant, because death depended upon body weight tightening the noose around the neck. A slight improvement was having the condemned person on a ladder or cart, and having this removed to hang him, but the big breakthrough would not come for centuries.

One immediate improvement was cosmetic, at best. This was a special belt with straps to hold the wrists and control the prisoner's struggling. After awhile, executioners decided that binding the condemned person's ankles was also worthwhile, to limit struggling, and this became part of the procedure.

During the early Nineteenth century, the technique of dropping the condemned to allow the rope to break his neck began to be popular. At first, the knot was placed behind the head, in the "occipital" position. This required a fairly long drop, as much as 14 feet, and often resulted in decapitation. Having the head taken off by the drop was aesthetically objectionable to fastidious executioners and their masters, and the "submental" knot was the result. This locates the knot under the ear, so that when the prisoner drops, the rope pulls sideways at the end of the drop, breaking the neck immediately.

Calculation of the optimum drop distance was long a subject for speculation and guesswork. However, the calculations are today very refined, and the U. S. Army has published a drop chart for people of various weights. (See chart on page 40.)

These drops are calculated to break the neck cleanly, but without severing the head from the body.[3] Unfortunately, decapitation is only one problem in execution by hanging.

At times, the prisoner has an especially muscular neck, and the spine does not break. This can result in the prisoner's slowly choking to death at the end of the rope. The expedient measure is to detail one or two soldiers to take hold of the prisoner's legs and to put their weights on them to hasten death. Another is loss of bowel and bladder function when the drop comes. Some prisoners even ejaculate by reflex action when the spine breaks. Anyone hanging onto the prisoner's legs is likely to find it unpleasant. This is also a messy problem for the clean-up squad.

120 lbs. or less-	8′1″	170 lbs.-	6′0″
125 lbs.-	7′10″	175 lbs.-	5′11″
130 lbs.-	7′7″	180 lbs.-	5′9″
135 lbs.-	7′4″	185 lbs.-	5′7″
140 lbs.-	7′1″	190 lbs.-	5′6″
145 lbs.-	6′9″	195 lbs.-	5′5″
150 lbs.-	6′7″	200 lbs.-	5′4″
155 lbs.-	6′6″	205 lbs.-	5′2″
160 lbs.-	6′4″	210 lbs.-	5′1″
165 lbs.-	6′2″	220 lbs. and over-	5′0″

Many executions by hanging in the American West were crude. Without a gallows, the expedient method was to tie the rope to a tree branch, sit the condemned man on a horse, and drive the horse out from under him. Another method was to stand him on a stool, and kick the stool away when it was time to carry out the sentence.

In one case, a seventeen-year-old boy was hanged at Little Rock, Arkansas, on January 8, 1864. Union troops had caught him with documents that proved he was a courier for Confederate spies, and he went on trial for his life. General Steele, presiding at the trial, made him an offer: to reveal the names of the spies in return for his life. The boy refused, and went to the gallows. He was small for his age, and when his body dropped, his neck didn't break, and he was writhing in the air until soldiers pulled on him until he died.[4]

Notable Hangings

Among the notable people hanged were Nathan Hale, an American hero. He died on September 27, 1776, after British troops had caught him with documents indicating that he was a Continental spy. His last words, "I regret that I have only one life to give for my country," became a part of American history and folklore.[5]

The U. S. Army used hanging after World War II for the disposal of various big-time German and Japanese "war criminals." Among those hanged on October 16, 1946, after the Nuremburg Trials, were Field Marshal Wilhelm Keitel, S.S. General Ernst Kaltenbrunner, and Field Marshal Alfred Jodl. Hermann Goering took his own life hours before the scheduled execution.

Other countries used the rope on Nazi war criminals. S.S. General Jurgen Stroop, who put down the Warsaw Ghetto uprising, went down at the end of a rope in Warsaw on September 8, 1951.[6]

The Nazis themselves used rope to terminate political undesirables. In some cases, they used piano wire for slow strangulation. Admiral Wilhelm Canaris, implicated in the plot to kill Hitler, came to his end in Flossenberg Concentration Camp on April 9, 1945, just a month before the war in Europe ended. Some accounts state that he was hoisted naked onto a hook, by a loop of piano wire, and filmed with a movie camera while he writhed in the air.

Thus we see that hanging can be humane or extremely cruel, depending on the method and the intentions of the executioner or his master. English hanging practices, and the American ones that followed, tended to produce death quickly and efficiently. Slow strangulation by hanging on a meat-hook, with a loop of piano wire around the neck, is torture.

We'll note similar themes in our next subject, beheading.

Sources

1. *Executions*, George V. Bishop, Los Angeles, CA, Sherbourne Press, 1965, p. 102.
2. *Ibid.*, p. 105.
3. *Procedure For Military Executions*, Department of the Army, Army Regulations 633-15, 1959, commercial reprint, p. 7, Section II, paragraph i.
4. *Death Penalty For Juveniles*, Victor L. Streib, Bloomington, IN, Indiana University Press, 1987, p. 79.
5. *Assassinations and Executions*, Harris M. Lentz, Jefferson, NC, McFarland and Company, Publishers, 1988, p. xvii.
6. *Ibid.*, p. 131.

7

Beheading

Chopping off the head is a classic method of execution, inherited from ancient times and still done today. Saudi Arabia is one country which still employs an executioner who chops the heads off the condemned with a heavy axe.

In some cases, even in the Twentieth Century, this primitive method serves to reinforce a primitive way of life, such as the execution of intellectuals in the Congo in 1964.[1] Anyone with more than a slight education was slated for a death sentence during that turbulent time.

The advantages of using an axe for beheading are that the instrument is simple, uses no electricity, doesn't require any chemicals, and has no moving parts to get out of order. Another advantage is that the method of use is simple, and anyone who needs an instruction manual doesn't deserve to be an executioner.

The disadvantage is that success depends very heavily upon individual skill, and there have been some very inept people serving as executioners. The goal is to sever the head with one blow, but novice or nervous executioners often botch this. It sometimes took a dozen or more strokes of the axe to sever the head. The Duke of Rothingham, executed in the Tower of London centuries ago, had very poor luck, and his executioner took 24 whacks to finish the job.[2]

Techniques of beheading varied, and we can divide them into two types: freehand and supported. A freehand beheading had the subject kneeling in front of the executioner with his head upright, and the executioner would take a roundhouse swing with sword or axe. A variant was to have the victim bow his head, while the executioner, standing to the side, delivered an overhead swing. There were problems with both methods. One was that the unsupported head and neck would often give with the blow, and the blade would not cut completely through. Another was that the subject would lose his nerve and would duck, throwing off the executioner's aim. This then required repeated blows.

The supported method used a chopping block, and the subject lay his head on it while the executioner set up for his swing. Having the head supported minimized movement, and enhanced the chances of a clean kill.

There were two types of chopping blocks; low and high. The low block was close to the ground, as the name implies, and was for prisoners churlish enough to struggle. Two guards sat on the prisoner's body, while the third would grasp his hair to put his neck on the stretch.[3] The high block allowed the prisoner to kneel, but required cooperation. The last time this technique saw use in England was for the beheading of Lord Lovat, in 1747.

This was perhaps appropriate, as the high block was the method generally reserved for the aristocracy.

Officially, beheading ceased to be the method of execution in England in 1747, but because the trend at the time was towards extreme cruelty in punishment, beheading continued to be a part of the execution ritual for almost 100 years afterward.[4] As executions were public at the time, judges and executioners combined to put on as gross a show as they could, presumably to deter anyone thinking of committing a crime. Therefore, the execution became a matter of one from column "A" and two from column "B." A typical sentence would be for the condemned person to be hanged, but while still alive, having to watch himself being disemboweled and his intestines burned. Afterwards, the executioner chopped off his head. This required that the hanging be slow-acting, and actually non-lethal, so as not to spoil the later stages of the execution. Subsequent stages would have been pointless if the condemned had not been alive and conscious to watch and suffer.

In the Twentieth Century, beheading with the sword or the axe has continued in some countries. Germany and Japan continued the practice, the Japanese using it on various prisoners of war. Some Americans captured by the Japanese during World War II suffered execution by decapitation, and these are the atrocities which lingered in the public mind.[5] Actually, some Americans ended up before a Japanese firing squad, because for reasons incomprehensible to Western minds, Japanese execution practices were inconsistent. Members of the Doolittle Raid of April, 1942, wound up before a Japanese firing squad.

Beheading is still used in some Moslem countries, such as Saudi Arabia. This country still has capital punishment for various crimes, and chopping off the head is the answer to murder, adultery, and various other acts which Moslems consider serious. Lesser offenses, such as stealing, call for amputation of the hands. This is done ceremonially, by the executioner's sword, not surgically in a hospital.

The Guillotine

Execution by beheading depended too heavily upon the skill of the executioner, and people concerned with speedy and humane executions sought quicker and more certain means. There had been experiments with mechanical beheading machines during the Middle Ages, but the climactic invention came during the years before the revolution, in France.

Drawing and quartering was the prescribed method in Royalist France, and this was, in the opinion of Dr. Joseph Ignace Guillotin, not a method fit for a civilized society. He felt that a mechanical knife, invented by another French doctor, Antoine Louis, was swifter and more humane. The reason that Guillotin's name went on the device, though, was that he pushed hard for its adoption, being a member of the Chamber of Deputies.

The Guillotine in its final form was the result of a research and development program much like the ones we find in the Twentieth Century. Once Dr. Louis had worked out the basic design, a call for bids on the prototype went out. A German harpsichord maker was the low bidder, and he put together a device which used a sharp blade falling vertically between two metal tracks to slice through the neck. A metal clamp held the heavy blade until the executioner pressed upon the "declic," or release.

Field-testing was the next step in the development, and the doctors tried the guillotine on some sheep. In this application, it worked well, slicing off their heads without any hang-ups. Human cadavers were next, and they procured three male corpses for the test. The blade neatly sliced off the heads of two corpses, but the third had a muscular neck, and this jammed the blade. The designers felt that an angled blade, and a longer drop, would solve the problem. With these modifications, the guillotine was ready for operational use.[6]

Nicolas-Jacques Pelletier, under sentence of death for stealing, took the first ride on April 25, 1792. This was an unqualified success, and between that date and June 8, 1793, 1,255 persons died by guillotine.[7] The guillotine was the final solution for many of the French nobility, because it came at the right moment to take a prominent place in the history of the French Revolution.

The guillotine was, from the start, a portable design, coming apart for easy transportation in a wagon. This also made preventive maintenance easy, for the executioner could inspect each component during assembly and take-down. If he saw undue wear, he could repair or replace the part.

The design evolved through the years. At first, there was only a board upon which the condemned person lay, with a semicircular slot for the neck at one end. This required forcing the prisoner to lie down, and stretching his neck into the slot. A later refinement was the clamp, which was a hinged piece of board, also slotted, which came down over the lower slot to hold the neck in place. The board gave way to a tipping board, known as a "bascule," which allowed the executioner to walk the prisoner up to the upright plank and fit his head into the slot. Once it was locked in, the executioner would tip the board over on its hinge to position the subject's neck below the blade. The final improvement was the automatic trip, in which the board cammed the release lever as soon as it was down in position.

Ever since beheading began, there was uncertainty regarding whether death was instantaneous, or the subject remained conscious, possibly even feeling pain, after the head parted from the neck. There had been several experiments to determine if life still existed in the severed heads. One bizarre effort was pumping dog's blood into the neck arteries to try to keep the head alive. A more reliable observer probably was Doctor Ronald Marcoux, who stood by and observed the falling heads during several executions.[8]

Marcoux noted that the eyelids fluttered open after he called the subject's name, and that the eyes seemed to stare at him as he was staring at the severed head. He claimed that the subject's eyes seemed to stare back at him with a "steady, knowing gaze."

French opinion was turning against capital punishment during the 1960s, and the guillotine was finally abolished under President Mitterand's administration.

Beheading, in its various forms, was gruesome enough. Man's ingenuity devised more gruesome methods, which we'll examine next before getting into more modern techniques of execution.

Sources

1. *New York Times*, October 4, 1964.
2. *Executions*, George V. Bishop, Los Angeles, CA, Sherbourne Press, 1965, pp. 117-118.
3. *Ibid.*, p. 121.
4. *Ibid.*, p. 122.
5. *Ibid.*, p. 124.
6. *Ibid.*, p. 47.
7. *Ibid.*, p. 41.
8. *Ibid.*, pp. 40-44.

8

Execution Horrors

Various imaginative methods of inflicting death have seen use as both executioners and their employers sought to maximize the suffering of the condemned. In the days when execution was mainly a reprisal, inflicting maximum suffering was a legitimate objective.

It's good practice for a person to be happy in his work. Adjusting to one's work, and even enjoying it, make for a well-integrated life. However, as we shall see in this and subsequent chapters, some executioners came to enjoy their duties too much.

Drawing and quartering was one extremely painful way to die. The executioner would tie the wrists and ankles of the condemned person to four powerful horses, each heading in a different direction. A touch of the whip would start them off, and the tension on the ropes would tear the prisoner apart.

It wasn't always neat, however, and during the execution of a man who had tried to assassinate the French king, Louis XV, the executioner had to finish the job by using a knife to cut though the ligaments.[1]

Sexual Thrills During Execution

Some people use the word "sadistic" when they mean "cruel." The two are not the same. Cruelty means inflicting pain or suffering. Sadism has to do with enjoying it.

One documented case of sadistic sexual perversion was Nero's voyeurism during the burning alive of Marcus Caius. Nero was apparently not only a sadist, but bisexual. Nero had his soldiers put the condemned man into the cavity of a bronze bull, after being flayed until his skin hung in strips. Once Caius was locked in, a slave lit the fire underneath the belly pan. Meanwhile, Sporus, Nero's Nubian slave, began sexually stimulating him. As the flames climbed higher, Nero had Sporus perform fellatio on him, timing it so that his climax came as Caius died, according to this source.[2]

During the Spanish Inquisition, families of condemned prisoners were very vulnerable to exploitation by corrupt jailers. Attractive females would be persuaded to have sex with corrupt officials in the hope that it would save their husbands or brothers from execution. Some officials would take advantage of female prisoners. A special technique, known by the French term of "Peine Forte et Dure," (strong and hard pain) was to spread-eagle the prisoner between metal rings set into the floor, and to pile flat rocks on her until the weight interfered with breathing. With enough weights piled on, death was inevitable. However, some of the more degenerate guards and officials would rape these women, as they'd discovered that the weight of the rocks constricted the vagina, providing heavier friction to the penis.[3]

The Garrote

The garrote, according to one account, developed as a merciful way of ending the suffering of a prisoner tortured by breaking on the wheel.[4] Allegedly, when the executioner had rolled the wheel, with the prisoner tied to its rim, around the town enough and broken every bone in his body, he could strangle the tortured man with a cord passed through a hole in the rim.

More likely, though, the garrote developed as a logical outgrowth of rope strangling, a technique used by Indian "Thuggees" and other hard-core types. The first formal garrote was a strong cord passed through a hole in a post. This made it simple to sit the prisoner in front of the post and strangle him by pulling on the cord. It didn't take much ingenuity to take the next step, tying the cord's ends to form a loop and twisting a stick through the loop for leverage. This allowed the executioner to apply pressure in carefully controlled increments, adapting the garrote as an instrument of torture.[5]

A sidelight to the garrote is that constriction of the neck often causes release of the bladder and bowels, and even penile erection through reflex action. This may have led to another perverted use of this method.[6]

Modern improvements on the garrote were substituting a metal band and screw-tightening mechanism for the cord, and using a couple of innovations to lessen the prisoner's suffering. One was the double band, which allegedly dislocates the spinal cord and thereby ends the prisoner's suffering. The other is the metal band with a blade at the back, which cuts the spinal cord when the executioner takes up the slack. This, too, allegedly speeds death.[7]

The garrote has seen use in other countries, such as Austria. As late as the Nineteenth Century, condemned criminals were executed by strangulation with a rope. The reported slow stranglings of Admiral Canaris, and others who plotted against Adolf Hitler, by piano wire, is a variation of the garrote theme.

Entombment

An ancient method of execution, designed for maximum public exposure, is encasing the condemned person in wet clay or cement, and leaving it to dry, trapping him until death from thirst, starvation, exposure, or exhaustion. One of the earliest recorded applications of this method was against captured members of bandit bands in Asia. When caravan guards captured one of the Mongol raiders, they would dig a pit, improvise a cement mix with soil, straw, and water, and bury the bandit up to his neck, watching while the mixture hardened. They would leave him there both as a warning and as a signpost.[8]

Entombment has also seen application in other locales. Thick walls surrounding a city often had cavities designed for entombment. Prisoners would actually form part of the wall, only their heads exposed, and they would take days to die.

Death of a Thousand Cuts

This is an oriental method, designed to inflict the maximum pain before extinction of life. Execution of a thief, for example, would begin with the thief tied to a cross. The executioner would cut off both hands at the wrist with a sharp knife, after which an assistant would cauterize the wounds with a flaming torch to stop the bleeding. The executioner would then make long cuts on the prisoner's body, from shoulders to feet, using a very sharp knife. None of these cuts were deep, or even life-threatening, as the purpose was to inflict maximum pain.[9]

Burning to Death

Burning at the stake wasn't the only method of execution by heat. In ancient Babylon, in the time of Hammurabi, the barbecue pit was the instrument of execution. Soldiers would tie the prisoner up and throw him into the flaming pit. This both carried out the sentence and disposed of the body.[10]

During a brief period in the Fifteenth Century, some executions by par-boiling took place in England. Soldiers would suspend the prisoner over a suitably large iron pot of water, and when it was boiling, they'd cut the rope and let him fall. They then stood by with long poles in case the prisoner tried to pull himself out by clambering over the rim of the pot.

Doubtless, other methods of torturing a condemned prisoner to death have existed. Documented cases describe more variants than we can list here. The modern trend is, however, towards quicker and more painless methods of execution. There's no guarantee that throwbacks cannot occur. Surely some regimes, and their executioners, are so perverted that they actively seek to inflict pain as a bonus during an execution.

A method that comes to us from the earliest days of firearms is execution by shooting. This can be quick, and less painful than most of the methods we've studied up to now.

Sources

1. *Executions*, George V. Bishop, Los Angeles, CA, Sherbourne Press, 1965, p. 45.
2. *Ibid.*, pp. 62-69.
3. *Ibid.*, pp. 95-96.
4. *Ibid.*, pp. 126-128.
5. *Ibid.*, p. 129.
6. *Ibid.*, p. 129.
7. *Ibid.*, p. 130.
8. *Ibid.*, p. 144.
9. *Ibid.*, p. 146.
10. *Ibid.*, pp. 151-152.

9

Shooting

Death by shooting is the mode in many countries of the world, and it's one choice in Utah, one of the few American states that offers condemned prisoners a choice in the manner of execution. The other state using the firing squad is Idaho, which like Utah, also offers a choice of death by injection.[1] A firing squad is often the preferred method in the military, partly because firearms are convenient, and partly because of the macho image. "Dying like a man" is still important to people who wear uniforms, and there seems to be something unmanly about a lethal injection or an electric chair.

The firing squad is also the manner prescribed in the Soviet Union, for both civil and military crimes. Other countries, such as Thailand, also use firing squads.

Utilitarian Execution

The simplest method of inflicting death with a gun is a shot to the back of the head or neck. This is the method used in public executions in the People's Republic of China today, with the condemned person made to kneel while the executioner places the barrel of the pistol to his head from behind. In Nazi Germany, the "genickschuss," or neck-shot, was one way of quickly and efficiently disposing of people who needed to be killed. The executioner would place the pistol barrel against the back of the neck, and the shot would sever the spinal cord.

The shot in the head is also a feature of American gangland "execution" killings. When the police find a body with hands tied behind the back, and one or more bullet holes in the head or neck, they conclude that it was a planned execution.

The Firing Squad

The method of conducting a military firing squad execution as prescribed by U.S. Army regulations is similar to those used by other countries. The court-martial or military command appoints an officer to take charge of the execution. He is responsible for gathering all of the people and materials needed and for delegating command of the actual execution to a junior officer.[2]

The firing squad is usually a scratch force, collected from whatever soldiers are available, or if a detail of military police is on the scene, from their number. By current regulations, the firing squad consists of eight men and one sergeant.[3] They rehearse the procedure until it's correct to the officer's satisfaction.

The officer in charge arranges the other details, such as selecting a suitable place of execution, having a stout post erected, and ensuring a solid backstop for the bullets. He oversees the loading of eight rifles, one to three of which, by regulation, may have blanks in their chambers. The escort party, which brings the prisoner to the execution post, consists of four men armed with rifles and one sergeant with a pistol.

Preparing the prisoner for execution is simple. He wears whatever clothing is suitable, but if it's a U.S. uniform, the officer sees to it that no insignia remain on the uniform. In the cell or holding area, the escort party binds the prisoner's wrists to his waist, using a specially designed strap to hold the hands at the front or at the back. They then take the prisoner, accompanied by a chaplain if he wishes, to the execution post. There, the officer in charge notifies the prisoner that he may make a last statement, if he wishes.

The sergeants of the escort and execution squads tie the prisoner to the post, using straps at the waist and ankles. They place a generously cut black hood over his head, and step back. The medical officer places a paper disc over the prisoner's heart and steps back.

Once everybody's clear of the target area, the officer gives the commands:

READY means that the soldiers take off their safeties.

AIM means that they aim at the paper target.

FIRE is the command for all to fire at once.

The officer and the doctor then examine the prisoner, and if life still remains, the sergeant of the firing squad comes forward to administer the "coup de grace," or mercy shot, aiming just above the ear.

It's not always as neat. In one execution in Utah, in 1951, a condemned man was shot, but on the wrong side of the chest, and he died from loss of blood.[4] Apparently, Utah executions have no provision for a coup de grace.

The Blank Cartridge

One of the persistent myths about firing squads is that one of the guns has a blank cartridge to create doubt about each member's role in actually killing. This has appeared in otherwise authoritative works.[5] It's true that, by most procedures, an officer loads each weapon out of sight of the firing squad and puts a blank cartridge in one of the weapons. However, anyone familiar with firearms knows that a blank produces far less recoil than a live round, and that the soldier who receives the blank knows without doubt that he did not fire a live round.

The Shooting of Private Slovik: An Actual Example

This noted case took place in 1944 and 1945, during some of the hottest fighting in Western Europe. Private Eddie Slovik, U.S. Army, deserted and was recaptured by the Army. The court-martial sentenced him to death, and the sentence was carried out at about 10 in the morning, January 31, 1945, at St. Marie aux Mines, in Eastern France.[6]

The execution site was the garden of a private house on a remote sidestreet. The garden had a high masonry wall, which would stop bullets. As an additional safeguard, army men built a wooden barrier in front of the stone wall, to catch ricochets. In front of the barrier was an upright execution post, made of "six by six," and six feet high. A large spike was at shoulder level to support the condemned after the shooting. Army personnel also prepared a "collapse board," to hold him up in case he was unable to stand. An officer procured a black hood from a civilian source.

For this execution, there were three medical officers, the senior of whom took the time to instruct the firing squad regarding the position of the heart. One of the troopers suggested that the doctor attach a piece of paper as an aiming point, but the doctor turned this down, feeling it was theatrical.

Regulations governing executions by firing squad were slightly different then, and one of the differences was that the detail could have as many as twelve men. Another difference was that only one of the rifles might contain a blank. Regulations also didn't provide for a coup de grace. If the prisoner wasn't dead after the first try, an officer would reload the rifles and the firing squad would deliver another volley.

The twelve riflemen were allegedly among the best shots in the division. Because the shooting was so unusual, they got "pep talks" from the commanding general and various other officers, including the Catholic chaplain. Slovik was Catholic, and as a part of standard operating procedure, the chaplain heard his confession, said a mass for him, and gave him absolution for his sins.

A sergeant tied Slovik's hands with nylon cord before moving him out to the post. At the post, the officer in charge read the execution order to him, and asked if he had any last statement to make. Slovik had nothing to say, and the sergeants tied his ankles together, and bound him to the post with web belts, hooked over the spike at the back of the post. Once Slovik was securely fastened to the post, a sergeant put the black hood on his head.

The lieutenant in charge of the firing squad marched them into the garden, and after they took their positions, the officer in charge of the execution ordered: "Squad, ready, aim, fire!"

Slovik slumped, and the medical officer walked up to him to ascertain if he was dead. Witnesses saw Slovik writhe at least twice. There was an awkward pause. Not one bullet had hit its target, Slovik's heart. The lieutenant in charge of the firing squad began reloading the rifles, in case a second volley became necessary. By the time he had finished, the doctor had pronounced Slovik dead.

In this case, the blank round was only a bad joke. The M-1 rifle has hardly any recoil when loaded with a blank. Also, because it depends upon gas pressure to cycle, the M-1 does not eject a blank cartridge.[7]

Shooting Spies and Traitors

Executions by firing squad have become fashionable for spies and traitors, especially in Europe. In the United States, the electric chair has been more popular. In Japan, beheading and the noose were in use during World War II.

In England, during World War I, the German spy, Carl Hans Lody, was shot by firing squad in the Tower of London, an ancient fortress on the shore of the Thames in downtown London.[8]

In some countries, such as France and Italy, spies face the firing squad. Traitors, though, are tied to the posts facing the other way, so that they're shot in the back to symbolize their dishonorable status.

The Firing Squad for Civil Crimes

The first execution in the United States after the Supreme Court gave capital punishment the green light was that of Gary Gilmore, in Utah, on January 17, 1977. Gilmore, who had been condemned for murder, sat down in the chair, guards tied his arms and legs, and the firing squad shot him to death.

As we've seen in an earlier chapter, condemned prisoners have a choice of execution methods in some states. In Utah at the time, Gilmore had the choice between hanging and shooting. The rope must have appeared unattractive, so he chose shooting.

The Utah firing squad consists of five citizens positioned behind a stone wall with firing ports.[9] The condemned person is strapped to a straight-back chair in front of another wall and a backstop to absorb any bullets which miss or penetrate the prisoner. The prison doctor pins a paper target over the prisoner's heart. At the order, the riflemen fire. One of the cartridges is blank, but this is unlikely to leave any doubt in anyone's mind.

Field-Expedient Executions

During wartime, many executions take place close to the front lines, and occasionally within the front lines, as a means of dealing with desertion and cowardice. Both official regulations and unofficial procedure allow officers to use deadly force to maintain discipline. Officers carry handguns for enforcing discipline, as well as for personal defense. An officer may shoot a trooper who refuses to advance, as an example to others.

During hard battles, there are squads of military police behind the lines, to intercept deserters. Depending on the situation, deserters may find themselves being held for later court-martial, or facing a "drum-head" court-martial soon after apprehension.

During the Italian retreat, after the battle of Caporetto, in 1917, military police combed through columns of retreating troops, seeking soldiers who had become separated from their units. This was prima facie evidence of desertion, and the military police immediately arrested these and brought them before field court-martials. The soldiers had the opportunity to explain why they were not with their units, and if the explanation was satisfactory, they were let go. If not, they immediately faced a firing squad.

Likewise during the German retreat from France in 1944 and 1945. German military police checked out retreating troopers to ensure that they were retreating under orders, as part of a unit, and not striking out on their own. Any deserters caught were either shot on the spot or hanged from a nearby lamp-post.

Mass Executions

During World War II, Nazi mobile execution squads, composed of S.S. men, roamed the Eastern Front. These "Einsatzgruppen," or "Action Groups," had the task of liquidating groups of people to help the war effort. In some cases, the Action Group troopers shot members of partisan bands, as a service for the conventional armed forces. Sometimes, they would shoot the entire population of a village as reprisal for guerrilla actions.

An Action Group consisted of only a few hundred men. The entire strength of the four Action Groups, labeled "A," "B," "C," and "D," was only 3,000 men combined. Each was under the command of a general in the S.S. and had its own transport, although it drew upon the resources of the local army group for supplies.

Local army commanders had no reservations about keeping the Action Groups well-supplied. The S.S. men took on the dirty jobs, which otherwise army troopers might have had to do. The war in Russia was noted for its brutality, and the Geneva Convention often didn't apply. Shooting civilians, a rare event on other fronts, was commonplace in the East.

Mass executions required special procedures to make them cost-effective. The first step was to round up a working party, consisting of local civilians, to dig a large ditch. In some cases, the ones to dig the ditch were the first to be shot, although the S.S. didn't tell them that. With the ditch complete, S.S. troopers would collect the condemned people and line them up at the edge of the ditch. Shooting would then begin, either by volleys from rifles, or with machine-guns, depending on what was available. The bodies would fall into the ditch and the commander might or might not delegate a trooper to walk the ditch to make sure all were dead before burial began. Another working party would fill in the ditch.

Some Action Group commanders had problems with their men. Shooting civilians, including women and children, resulted in excessive alcohol consumption, and some troopers could carry out their duties only when half-drunk. Others enjoyed it, and commanders had to be watchful and weed out those who appeared to adjust to the duty too easily. One commander reported that, at the first sign that a trooper was becoming sexually excited by the shooting, he would transfer him out of the unit.[10]

There have been other mass shootings during the Twentieth Century, but the reason that those on the Eastern Front are so noted is that they were so well-documented. During the Russian Revolution, there were also mass executions, but the Russians were not as meticulous about recording when and where, and how many. Therefore, historians can only estimate how many people were shot to death.

Likewise, there were mass shootings during the 1930s, both in the Spanish Civil War and in the Japanese-Chinese skirmishes, but the participants didn't keep good records. The Katyn Forest mass execution of Polish officers by Soviet troops was long in dispute, because during the war it was more convenient to believe that the Germans had done it and were trying to cover it up by blaming it on the Russians.

Expedient Executions

During war, the order occasionally goes out: "Take no prisoners." This is always informal, spread only by word-of-mouth, for obvious reasons.

The take no prisoners rule isn't necessarily because of cruelty, but the result of the exigencies of battle. There may not be enough troopers to guard prisoners of war. There also may be no place to put them or not enough food to feed them. This means that any prisoners face immediate disposal.

Americans have also shot prisoners. This wasn't necessarily to produce an atrocity, such as the one at My Lai, in Vietnam. During the Anzio landing, in 1943, the fighting was desperate and American troops were pinned down on a small beach-head, with German guns on the heights overlooking the beach and the harbor. An American soldier recalls what happened to prisoners in his sector:

"I was in the company command post when some guys brought in a couple of Germans. The company commander interviewed them, asked them where they were from and how many men in their unit. After he got the information he wanted from them, he took me aside. He told me that there was no room for prisoners, and we barely had enough food for ourselves. That was why the word had come down; 'no prisoners.' He told me to take another guy with me, and take the two prisoners out back, give them a cigarette, and shoot them."[11]

During war emergencies, civilians come under martial law, and both military and police have extraordinary powers. They may use deadly force to stop panic, looting, sabotage, and any other action harmful to the war effort or to the public safety. In war-time Germany, after the British and Americans began bombing German cities, there were mass evacuations. At that time, people could, and did, leave their luggage on the floor in train stations, if they had to go to the ticket counter, toilet or the station buffet. This was because there was a summary death penalty for anyone stealing luggage. One German recalls:

"A police officer caught a thief making off with luggage, and he took him around the corner, down a hallway. There, out of sight of the main waiting room, he shot him with his pistol."[12]

Shooting never caught on very well in the United States. The gas chamber, however, became fairly popular, and this is what we'll study next.

Sources

1. *Information Please Almanac*, 1989, p. 801.
2. *The Executioner's Handbook, Procedure For Military Executions*, Department of the Army, Army Regulations 633-15, 1959, commercial reprint, p. 2, Section I, paragraphs b and c.
3. *Ibid.*, p. 4, Section II, paragraph c.
4. *Executions*, George V. Bishop, Los Angeles, CA, Sherbourne Press, 1965, p. 34.
5. *Ibid.*, p. 34.
6. *The Execution of Private Slovik*, William Bradford Huie, New York, Dell Publishing Company, 1970.
7. *Ibid.*, p. 223.
8. *Cry Spy!*, Burke Wilkinson, Englewood Cliffs, NJ, Bradbury Press, 1969, pp. 34-35. The account in this book claims that Lody refused a blindfold, but it's uncertain whether this is truth or legend from a time when spies were recklessly romanticized.
9. *Executions*, George V. Bishop, p. 34.
10. Report by Major-General Otto Ohlendorf to S.S. Headquarters, 1943.
11. Statement to the author by a former U. S. Army trooper who was at Anzio.
12. Statement to the author by a man who had grown up in Germany during the war.

10

Execution by Gas

The first execution by lethal gas took place in the United States in 1924, in Nevada, where this method had become legal in 1921. Execution by lethal gas was to replace the rope in that state, as a more humane way of putting a condemned person to death. The original idea had been to introduce the gas into the condemned person's cell as he slept, but it soon became clear that there were several practical difficulties with this plan. It was finally necessary to construct a hermetically sealed gas chamber, with a method of generating the gas once the prisoner was sealed inside.

Death by Gas: The Nuts and Bolts

The death chamber usually has windows, for the benefit of official witnesses. There's also a small aperture for a tube leading to a stethoscope strapped to the condemned person's chest. This allows a doctor to determine when the prisoner finally expires. In more modern times, the leads of an electrocardiograph are attached to the prisoner's chest.

The gas chamber is hermetically sealed, to protect the prison staff and witnesses from accidental release of gas. There may be an evacuation blower, to reduce air pressure in the gas chamber itself. This negative pressure is a further safeguard against leaks. A collateral effect, if the vacuum is high enough, is depriving the prisoner of oxygen, and this may induce drowsiness or unconsciousness before the gas hits.

The gas chamber may have one or two seats. Each is constructed of metal, and has straps attached to allow holding the prisoner securely to the seat. Under one chair is a bucket, which may be recessed into the floor. A solution of sulfuric acid is in this bucket, and there are two ways of filling it. One is manually, before the execution ceremony begins. A guard or technician pours the acid directly into the bucket. The other is remotely, with a pipe leading to a tank outside the gas chamber. The tank holds the acid, and after the prisoner is strapped in, a guard opens a valve, allowing the acid to flow into the bucket.

Above the bucket is a lever holding a cheesecloth bag full of cyanide "eggs." These are large pellets of sodium or potassium cyanide. Pulling a lever outside the gas chamber allows the bag of pellets to drop into the acid, where the compound turns into sodium or potassium sulfate, releasing hydrogen cyanide gas.

The prisoner is lightly dressed, because heavy clothing might trap some gas, making it hazardous for those removing the body.[1] After the guards strap him in, one may offer him a last word of advice. This is to take a deep breath after he hears the pellets drop, so that the gas may take effect quickly.[2] After the execution, an exhaust fan evacuates the gas, so that guards may remove the body.

Prisoners react differently to cyanide gas inhalation, depending on individual constitution and circumstances. Some fall unconscious quickly, and have a slight muscle spasm before dying. Others, especially those who hold their breath to postpone the end, suffer more. They may gasp, choke, and undergo the effects of asphyxia, including convulsions.[3] Some lose bowel or bladder control.

Awkward Executions

Execution by gas doesn't always go smoothly. A murderer named Riley had been sentenced to death for a killing he'd committed during an armed robbery in Los Angeles. When it came time to walk down the hall to the execution chamber, he fought his guards all the way. Still kicking and screaming, he resisted while guards strapped him into the chair in the gas chamber. The guards closed the door of the gas chamber, but before the pellets dropped into the acid, he slipped his hands and feet free of the straps. Getting up, he pounded at the door, demanding that they open it. The guards entered once more, and strapped him in again, but once they were out the door he got loose again. The pellets went into the acid, and the gas started coming out. Within a few minutes, cyanide gas had overcome him, and he lay dead on the floor.[4]

Another prisoner, Jimmy Lee Gray, was strapped to a chair behind which a steel pole ran from floor to ceiling. Gray repeatedly slammed his head back into the pole after the fall of the pellets.[5]

At times, a celebrated case can bring the entire institution into question or disrepute. Caryl Chessman died in California's gas chamber on May 2, 1960, after 12 years of fighting the system. Chessman, with an intelligence quotient of 138, was a petty thug who preyed on couples parked in lover's lanes. Flashing a red light, to suggest that he was a police officer, he would abduct young women and rape them. His modus operandi earned him the sobriquet of "red light bandit."[6]

Under California's "little Lindbergh" law at that time, kidnapping made one eligible for the death penalty, even if the victim survived. Chessman was no doubt guilty, and did not have much public sympathy during the early years of his efforts to cheat the gas chamber. One point that worked in his favor was that he'd never been convicted of murder, only kidnapping. To many people, the extreme penalty seemed too severe for someone who had not actually taken human life.

Chessman and his lawyer, George Davis, worked together to generate a series of appeals to string out the proceedings as long as possible. They sent appeals to both state and federal courts, and as each failed, they managed to find new grounds for yet another appeal. This fast footwork bought Chessman the time to make yet another appeal, this one to the court of public opinion.

Chessman was literate enough to write a book, *Cell 2455 Death Row*, which brought his side of the case into public view in a way no news account could. *Cell 2455 Death Row* is an indictment of the United States' criminal justice system, which Chessman claimed was unfeeling and unfair to people accused of crimes. Of course, Chessman argued against the death penalty, although he had remarkably little to say about the suffering he'd caused his victims. His book, and the one to follow, were examples of deft manipulation of public opinion by a clever criminal and propagandist.

Chessman's books were translated into several languages, and he found a constituency on foreign shores. Many people were convinced that Chessman's death sentence was merely evidence of the brutality of American justice. During the last weeks before his execution, the editor of a French newspaper stated that he'd gotten 50,000 letters calling for the sparing of Chessman's life. The editor of the Vatican newspaper, *Osservatore Romano*, called for a reprieve. Other individuals and groups, in the United States and elsewhere, joined the effort.

Chessman's lawyers, ready to make every effort to muddy the issue, made a belated announcement that they were looking for another suspect whom, they alleged, resembled the "red light bandit" more than Chessman did. The new suspect never turned up, and they prepared another set of final appeals. They filed a new petition with the California Supreme Court, and when this did not get Chessman reprieved, they tried a federal judge just before the execution time. The judge's secretary tried to telephone the prison, as the judge wanted an hour to read the petition, but got the wrong number on the first try. On the second try, she got through, but heard that the gassing had already begun. This was the real-life incident upon which one of the final scenes in the motion picture was patterned.

Some years earlier, a man named Henry McCracken went insane while waiting on San Quentin's death row. A panel of psychiatrists stated that he was not fit for execution in this state. Prison officials arranged for a quick series of electro-shock treatments to bring him back to sanity long enough for a legal execution.[7] A few years before that, another death row inmate, Robert Pierce, cut his throat with a piece of glass just before his execution. It was necessary to rush him to the gas chamber so that the state could kill him, rather than let him die by his own hand.[8]

Execution by gas, once the trendy method, is on the way out because it requires too much capital investment in special equipment, and there is a serious public relations problem associated with gas execution. Another method, employed in America for over two decades longer than gas, is electrocution, and this is the technique we'll study next.

Sources

1. *Capital Punishment*, Edited by Thomas Draper, New York, The H. W. Wilson Company, 1985, p. 70.
2. *Ibid.*, p. 72.
3. *Reviving The Death Penalty*, Gary E. McCuen and R. A. Baumgart, Hudson, WI, GEM Publications, 1985, p. 24.
4. *Capital Punishment*, p. 73.
5. *Ibid.*, p. 150.
6. *When Men Play God: The Fallacy of Capital Punishment*, Eugene B. Block, San Francisco, CA, Cragmont Publications, 1983, pp. 136-141.
7. *Executions*, George V. Bishop, Los Angeles, CA, Sherbourne Press, 1965, p. 155.
8. *Ibid.*, p. 156.

11

Electrocution

People had long been dimly aware that electricity, somehow, could be dangerous. Accounts of people and animals struck by lightning told of strange effects, and even death, resulting from accidental jolts of high-voltage juice. However, during the late Nineteenth Century, in the United States, deliberate experimentation with electricity for executions began. This was the latest effort in the search for tidiness in the death chamber.

At the time, hanging was the most widely used method of putting condemned criminals to death in this country. As we've seen, hanging had its problems, usually centering around slow strangulation or decapitation. New York State legislators, in particular, were distressed by a recent messy hanging which some of them had witnessed.[1]

The Dawn of Electrocution

Technology came to the rescue, in the rivalry of two electric power companies. One company, trying to sell the merits of Direct Current to the American people, laid on a traveling road show that demonstrated the lethal effects of alternating current on hapless test animals. This was in an era when animal welfare leagues either did not exist or did not have the moral force that they do today.

New York legislators realized that they had a new and potentially more humane and foolproof method of execution in electricity, and they passed a law adopting this method for New York State. A quick-witted individual coined the neologism "electro-cution" for the new method, and the first such execution took place on August 6, 1890, at Auburn Prison.

William Kemmler, originally sentenced to hang, had the dubious honor of getting the first test drive of the new "hot seat." There was some doubt regarding whether or not the new method of execution would actually work, and kill Kemmler by itself. To guard against the possibility of the current merely stunning him without killing, officials scheduled his autopsy immediately following the session in the seat, in an autopsy room next door to the death chamber. A special instruction to the coroner was to remove Kemmler's heart and brain, as a safeguard against his not being quite dead at the end of the electrocution.[2]

One electrode was on top of Kemmler's head. The other was attached to his back. When the executioner turned on the current, Kemmler's body jerked and the chair, which wasn't adequately anchored, began to rock. This horrified some spectators, who thought that Kemmler was struggling to break free. Davis, the executioner, kept the current on for five minutes, to make sure of the effect. When the current went off, Kemmler was apparently not quite dead, in the estimation of the witnesses. The executioner turned on the current once more, administering a series of short shocks to finish the job.[3]

The autopsy showed that Kemmler was thoroughly cooked, and his brain blackened from the heat. This showed conclusively exactly how electrocution worked, for those who had been uncertain. The shock of the current merely renders the subject unconscious, and may stop the heart and lungs. The body's resistance to the current produces heat, and this makes the effect permanent. It's the cooking that kills.

Electrocution Setbacks

Other electrocutions took place, most going fairly smoothly, until William Taylor died on July 27, 1893. The first 2,000 volt current went through Taylor, and his skin color became ruddy from the heat. After the executioner turned the current off, his body relaxed. The executioner turned the switch on again, but nothing happened, as one of the leads had broken. Taylor's body was still moving slightly.

This was a serious development, and it became necessary to repair the chair before the execution could proceed. Guards unstrapped Taylor from the chair and carried him into the next room, where doctors administered morphine and chloroform to keep him pain-free and unconscious until the state could finish killing him by the prescribed means. After 15 minutes, the chair was ready, and guards strapped Taylor into it once more for the rest of the program. This time, it worked well, and Taylor was soon definitely dead.[4]

Mechanical difficulties are not the only problems. Some candidates for the "hot seat" find themselves lacking in moral fiber when it comes time to walk that last mile. When John Spenkelink went to the chair in Florida, on May 25, 1979, it took six guards to drag him from his cell to the electric chair. He'd already gotten his last shave, to allow free passage of the electric current into his skull, and his pants leg was slit for the electrode. By this time, the procedure was well-established, and experience had shown that it was best if the electric current traversed the entire body, from the top of the head to the ankle.

Guards strapped him into the chair and attached a black muzzle to his neck and chin. A towel held his head to the back of the chair. A guard put a wet sponge on top of his head and lowered the metal dome to make contact. Another put a black hood over his face, to spare witnesses the sight of his biting his tongue when the current hit. One wire went to his ankle, and the other to his head. The executioner threw the switch, and Spenkelink got 2,000 volts through his body. After the third jolt, he was pronounced dead.[5]

Shortly after midnight, on December 12, 1984, Alpha Otis Stephens went to the electric chair in Georgia. It was a typical execution. An initial current of 2,080 volts went through his body for two minutes. He was still breathing, and the execution was interrupted for six minutes to allow his body to cool long enough for a doctor to examine him to verify that he was still alive. His body had warmed to about 140 degrees. The warden ordered another jolt, and this one finished Stephens.[6]

Preparation For Death

There are other aspects of electrocution that are not documented, but they are nevertheless real. One is the manner in which officials handle the prisoner who struggles all the way, and fights the guards who try to take him down the hall. This can happen whatever the method of execution, and in many cases the procedure is similar. Some hours before the execution, guards walk the prisoner to a special holding cell or room near the execution chamber. This may be a small room immediately next to the death chamber, or just down the hall. The important point is that it's isolated from other cells on death row, and out of sight and hearing of any witnesses to the execution.

At least two guards remain with the prisoner, and form an estimate of how troublesome he's likely to be when the moment comes. If the subject appears likely to struggle, a special procedure comes into effect. When it's time to escort him to the execution chamber, several guards enter and pin his arms, while an especially strong guard punches him in the solar plexus to induce collapse. This is usually enough to make him tractable until they can get him into the death chamber, but if this isn't enough, a couple of kicks to the testicles will subdue him. With the fight knocked out of him, he's easier to handle. Once he's firmly strapped into the chair, it doesn't matter if he recovers enough to fight: he's only got a few seconds until the electric current puts him down for the last time.

This softening-up procedure is the real reason why some prisoners come into the death chamber completely supported by their escorts, legs dragging behind them. Others can walk under their own power, but lose bowel and bladder control on the way.

In any case, the jolt of the powerful current usually results in urination or defecation in the chair. This is why there's a clean-up period afterwards, with an orderly washing down the chair with detergent and ammonia solution to prepare it for the next prisoner. Some prison administrators try to forestall this by tying a strong rubber tube, or fastening a clamp around the prisoner's penis. This stopgap measure doesn't work with females, and there's no practical way to stop involuntary defecation.

Photographs

Photographs are forbidden, but in one notorious case, a photograph of an electrocution was on Page 1 of many newspapers. When Ruth Snyder and Judd Gray went to the electric chair in 1927, a reporter had a small camera strapped to his ankle. When the current hit Ruth Snyder, he lifted his pants leg and tripped the cable release.[7]

Is Electrocution Painless?

Some doubt the humaneness of electrocution. One disturbing aspect for witnesses is the prisoner's convulsions. With the first jolt, the back arches and the prisoner appears to be trying to jump out of the chair. Although a hood keeps them from seeing the facial contortions, and the biting of the tongue, the sight is gruesome to certain witnesses. The skin turns red, because the prisoner is literally being cooked in his own juices. After the first jolt, the executioner turns off the current and the prisoner's body relaxes in the chair. At this time, if he's not dead yet, he may gasp and wheeze for breath.

One commentator feels that the prisoner may be fully conscious despite the heavy jolt of current.[8] Other evidence, however, shows that this is extremely unlikely. Experiences of people who have received electric shock therapy have been unanimous: there's loss of consciousness the moment the current comes. Some recall seeing a flash of light before their eyes, but none claimed to have remained conscious. This is significant, because the current used in electro-shock is only about 110 to 150 volts, a far lower amperage than that used in electrocution.

Those watching a patient receive electro-shock therapy, however, are as likely to be horrified as those watching an electrocution, if the classic method is used. The patient lies on a gurney, and an assistant attaches moistened electrodes to his temples. Another places a short length of rubber hose, or other suitable device, between his teeth, and holds his jaw shut to prevent biting of the tongue. Other assistants hold the patient down, against the convulsions which the current will produce.

Although the current lasts about one second, at most, the patient immediately loses consciousness, and his body tenses, with the back arched and the arms and legs trying to jackknife. After a few seconds, the entire body relaxes, and the spasms begin. These convulsions continue for about thirty seconds, until the patient once more relaxes. It's then necessary to turn him onto his side to allow saliva to drain from his mouth, otherwise he'd drown in his own spit. The unconscious state becomes more like normal sleep, and the patient awakens a few minutes to an hour afterwards. Hollywood has produced several versions of electro-shock treatment in films, the most realistic being Jack Nicholson's performance in *One Flew Over the Cuckoo's Nest.*

Today, electro-shock sees little use, and the custom in the United States is to anesthetize the patient before pushing the button. The patient also receives a dose of Pavulon, or Anectine, to relax the muscles and reduce the intensity of the convulsions. Depending on the dose, convulsions may be totally suppressed.

The Rosenberg Case

In one noted case, electrocution was part of an effort to obtain additional information about a Soviet spy ring in the United States. This was the notorious Rosenberg case.

Julius and Ethel Rosenberg were part of a large Soviet spy ring operating in the United States since before World War II. During the war, and shortly after its end, employees of the Manhattan District, the U.S. Army project developing the nuclear bomb, passed information about the design and construction of atom bombs to couriers working for the Soviet Military Intelligence Service.

Julius Rosenberg had boasted to his brother-in-law and fellow conspirator, David Greenglass, of the network of agents he ran in this country.[9] However, the network was starting to unravel, mainly because of efforts by U.S. Government code breakers. Around the end of the war, code breakers were able to start breaking into an accumulation of KGB messages, with the help of fragments of a Soviet code book bought from the Finns.[10] Decoded fragments of text hinted at a massive spy ring. This, and other information, led to the Rosenbergs. It appeared to the FBI that Julius had actually been the spy-master, with his wife

Ethel helping in the background, but they took advantage of the prospect of convicting her to put pressure on Julius to talk, and reveal his entire network. Indeed, one of the former FBI Agents central to the investigation has stated that this was precisely the result for which they hoped.[11]

Federal prosecutors went for the death penalty. As the case was being tried in New York, death would be by electrocution, as the federal government used local facilities whenever possible.

The trial itself depended on partial and flimsy evidence, because although Rosenberg was actually guilty as charged, the government was trying to save its secrets. Among these were classified data about atom bomb designs, and the fact that breaking of Soviet codes used during WWII was still continuing in the summer of 1951.[12] That escaping prosecution was contingent upon helping the government in its case was evident in the fact that Ruth Greenglass, David's wife, was not prosecuted at all, after she agreed to spill her knowledge to government agents and even to testify against her in-laws.

Some people believed that the government actually framed the Rosenbergs.[13] This viewpoint did not appear very plausible at the time, but today, in the light of what we know about code breaking, and the crucial need to keep from the Soviets the knowledge that we were reading their coded messages, it seems more likely.

FBI Director Hoover hoped that one or the other of the Rosenbergs would talk to save themselves, especially as they had two pre-teen sons whom their deaths would leave orphans. To this end, he sent Assistant Director Alan Belmont to Sing Sing Penitentiary on the morning of June 19, 1953.[14] This was fruitless, as both Rosenbergs went to their deaths silently, and sequentially, as Sing Sing had only one electric chair. Julius was pronounced dead at 8:05 P.M., and Ethel at 8:15.

Other Electrocutions

George Stinney was a black boy, aged 14 years and 8 months, when electrocuted for the murder of two white girls in South Carolina. Stinney stood five feet, one inch, and weighed 95 pounds when led to the execution chamber. Guards had to take up on straps designed to hold much larger bodies. As with adults, it took three jolts of current to kill him, and he died three minutes after the start of the execution. The mask, designed for an adult, was loose, and his face emerged from under it while the current was flowing.[15]

Some states, such as Mississippi, have portable electric chairs because the law requires that the executions take place in the county or parish of the trial. The executioner brought his portable chair to the Woodville Jail, where he adjusted the chair to fit two boys, aged 14, who had gotten the death sentence for murder. He adjusted the chair to the dimensions of the felons, and executed them one after the other on July 23, 1947.[16]

In one instance, an electrical failure caused a delay of a year between sessions in the death chamber. Willie Francis, 15 years old, was black and had been convicted of murder in Louisiana. On May 3, 1946, guards strapped Willie into the portable electric chair and placed the hood over his face. The executioner threw the switch, but all Francis got was a tickle, as a wire had burned out. He complained that the hood was smothering him, and the guards unstrapped him. His attorneys used this event as a basis for an appeal, stating that Francis was now in double jeopardy, and asked for the striking down of the death sentence.

After many months of legal maneuvering, Francis again got his execution date; June 7, 1947. This time, when he sat in the chair, the device did not fail, and Francis died.[17]

Electrocution Sidelights

In some states, there have been efforts to dilute the act of throwing the switch, comparable to loading one of the firing squad's rifles with a blank. In Georgia, for example, there are three guards detailed to pull switches, but only one switch is actually wired to the electric chair. The prison electrician changes the wiring each time, so that none of the three delegated to this job knows which had the live one.[18]

At times, electrocution of condemned killers has had political sidelights. Nicola Sacco and Bartolomeo Vanzetti were two Italian radicals who were convicted of a felony-murder during an armed robbery committed in Braintree, Massachusetts, in 1919. During this era, there were mass round-ups of Italian radicals because of various violent incidents. Although Sacco and Vanzetti stood trial and their conviction stood up under appeal, there was wide-spread feeling that they had been "railroaded" because of their political coloring. There were demonstrations on their behalf, and many books and articles written after their deaths, but they went to the electric chair on August 23, 1927.[19]

There are still hangups occurring during electrocutions, despite an entire century to refine and perfect the technique. A very recent incident took place during the execution of Jessie Joseph Tafero, who had been convicted of killing two police officers. On May 4, 1990, officials at the Florida State Prison in Starke, Florida, strapped Tafero into the electric chair. One of the steps was to place a sponge soaked in salt solution on top of his head to conduct the current. Press accounts speculated that the sponge, which replaced the natural sea sponge used for 21 previous electrocutions, was synthetic. When the 2,000 volts and 14 amps hit Tafero, the sponge dried out, and began smoking. Flames came out from under the black hood covering Tafero's face. Tafero was still breathing after the first jolt. Two more applications of current left him still breathing, and moving his head, but a fourth jolt suppressed all activity. Florida Department of Corrections spokesman Bob MacMaster stated that Tafero was dead after the first application, and that subsequent movement was involuntary.[20]

Electrocution, like the rope and the gas chamber, has seen less use in the United States during recent years. The trendy method which has been gaining on all three is lethal injection. This is what we'll analyze in the next chapter.

Sources

1. *Executions*, George V. Bishop, Los Angeles, CA, Sherbourne Press, 1965, p. 19.
2. *Ibid.*, pp. 18-19.
3. *Ibid.*, pp. 20-21.
4. *Ibid.*, pp. 21-23.
5. *Capital Punishment*, Edited by Thomas Draper, New York, The H. W. Wilson Company, 1985, p. 59.
6. *Ibid.*, p. 11.
7. *Executions*, George V. Bishop, p. 25.

8. *Reviving The Death Penalty*, Gary E. McCuen and R. A. Baumgart, Hudson, WI, GEM Publications, 1985, p. 23.
9. *The FBI-KGB War*, Robert J. Lamphere and Tom Schachtman, New York, Berkley Books, 1986, p. 192.
10. *Ibid.*, pp 80-101.
11. *Ibid.*, p. 238.
12. *Ibid.*, p. 260.
13. *Ibid.*, p. 265.
14. *Ibid.*, p. 278.
15. *Death Penalty For Juveniles*, Victor L. Streib, Bloomington, IN, Indiana University Press, 1987, p. 109.
16. *Ibid.*, p. 115.
17. *Ibid.*, pp. 113-114.
18. *When Men Play God: The Fallacy of Capital Punishment*, Eugene B. Block, San Francisco, CA, Cragmont Publications, 1983, pp. 88-89.
19. *Assassinations and Executions*, Harris M. Lentz, Jefferson, NC, McFarland and Company, Publishers, 1988, p. 53.
20. *Miami Herald* and Associated Press, May 5, 1990.

12

Lethal Injection

The latest trend in promoting tidy execution chambers is death by lethal injection, also known sarcastically as "death by anesthesia." Killing by the injection of drugs isn't new. The technology has existed as long as hypodermic needles, which first appeared during the last century. The New York State Legislature, when considering changing the mode of execution, discussed lethal injection before deciding on electrocution.[1]

Population Thinning in the Third Reich

One widespread use of lethal injections for killing was in the Third Reich during World War II, when German doctors implementing the "T-4 Program" eliminated people who were "unfit" by injections of phenol into the heart. The "unfit" included the incurably insane, the mentally retarded, and people who were hopelessly ill or crippled. The government set up a special assessment program, in cooperation with mental hospitals, institutions for the feeble-minded, and various hospitals housing the chronically ill. Medical review teams judged the chances of recovery on a case-by-case basis, and those who showed no promise either got their lethal injections on-site or after transfer to a clinic for the administration of such injections. Death certificates, however, never reflected the purposeful termination of life by government decree, perhaps to spare the relatives' feelings or to avoid negative publicity. A few euphemistic "causes" of death, such as "heart failure" or "pneumonia," seemed to serve repeatedly.

Lethal Injections in the U.S.

In the United States, there has not been a formal program for the termination of hopelessly handicapped people, but there have been occasional efforts by doctors to put terminally ill people to sleep. The January 8, 1988, issue of the *Journal of the American Medical Association* carried an account titled "It's Over, Debbie," relating how the anonymous author gave a young lady with terminal cancer a fatal injection to end her suffering.

During the 1970s, there developed an interest in a better, more tidy, and more certain method of execution. After many decades of experience with high-tech methods such as cyanide gas and electrocution, dissatisfaction had set in and there was agitation for a more "humane" method of seeing off the condemned. There were some ghastly stories regarding execution failures and botches.

This also came after the striking down of capital punishment by the U. S. Supreme Court. The basic problem was that there was no egalitarian method of setting death sentences, and the Chief Justices feared that people were receiving death sentences capriciously, instead of according to fixed guidelines. This set back capital punishment in the United States for several years, while states formulated new laws to pass the Supreme Court test.

Resumption of executions also depended upon good public relations, as there was a powerful "bleeding heart" movement concerned with the suffering of the condemned during execution. Electrocution produced convulsions while the current was passing through the body, and assurances that the subject was unconscious and not feeling any pain were unconvincing to some people. Likewise, execution by gas seemed inhumane to some, because unconsciousness was not immediate and the condemned often seemed to gag and cough when the cyanide gas first hit. There were also convulsions after loss of consciousness, before death ensued.

Beginnings

Oklahoma was the first state to adopt lethal injection to execute criminals, in 1977.[2] This may have been for reasons of economy. The cost of reconditioning the electric chair, or of building a new gas chamber, was perhaps too high for the legislature to afford. However, Texas was the first state actually to perform an execution in this manner, when Charlie Brooks was executed on December 7, 1982.

The Nuts and Bolts of Lethal Injections

The cost of lethal injection is small. There's very little required in equipment, unlike some other methods which use special fixtures to hold the condemned while he's being put to death.

Instead of a special-purpose chair, or an airtight chamber, the prisoner is strapped to a hospital gurney, and a conventional intravenous set-up serves to pass the drugs into his vein.

There are three drugs used together in most chemical executions: *Thiopental* is a quick-acting intravenous anesthetic that causes unconsciousness, *Pavulon* is similar to curare in action, a paralytic agent that stops breathing, and *Potassium chloride* stops the heart.[3]

The tube leading to the prisoner's vein begins in an adjacent room, where there is a container of saline solution dripping into it to carry the drugs used for execution. The requirements for the execution procedure vary with the state. In New Jersey, the law states that "Prior to the injection of the lethal substance, the person shall be sedated by a licensed physician, registered nurse, or other qualified personnel, by either an oral tablet or capsule or an intramuscular injection of a narcotic or barbiturate such as morphine, cocaine, or demerol."[4]

In other states, the entire mixture comes through the tube at once, like a massive cocktail. The person or people who push the plunger also vary from state to state. In New Jersey, doctors are specifically forbidden to administer the lethal drugs. In Montana, the person may be a physician, but not necessarily.[5] In some cases, there's a panel of executioners, two with syringes filled with a harmless solution and one with the lethal dose. All three press their plungers at the signal, and none know which of them actually did it.[6]

A condemned man named Charlie Brooks became the first to die by chemical execution, in Texas, in 1982. The prison doctor, Ralph Gray, examined his veins before the execution to ensure that injection was possible. He lay down on the gurney, allowed the execution technician to insert a needle in his vein, and waited for the chemicals to arrive. As soon as the lethal chemicals went into his bloodstream, Brooks closed his eyes, and within a few minutes expired peacefully. Seven minutes after the injection began, the prison doctor pronounced him dead.[7]

Pitfalls and Problems

It doesn't always happen that neatly. Indeed, one of the objections raised by the British Royal Commission that examined capital punishment in the early 1950s was that the prisoner would have to cooperate, at least enough to remain still while the executioner found a vein and inserted the needle.[8] Finding a vein can be tricky, and even with the prisoner's cooperation, it may not always be possible. Some people have smaller veins than others, and they're not always at the same distance from the surface of the skin.

A man named J. D. Autry committed a felony-murder in April, 1980, and after several sentencings, reprieves, and other delays, he finally ended up on the gurney on March 14, 1984. The warden asked him if he had any last words, and when he answered in the negative, gave the signal to begin. In the next room, the executioners pumped the lethal cocktail into the long tube that led to Autry's vein. It took him 10 minutes to die, and he complained of pain in his arm before losing consciousness.[9] One doctor, who examined Autry after the execution, stated that the process had taken so long because the tube leading to his arm was clogged. It's also possible that the needle missed the vein, or slipped out before the flow of chemicals began. This would have deposited the lethal cocktail in surrounding tissues, from where absorption into the bloodstream would have been much slower.

Raymond Landry was on the execution gurney in the state prison at Huntsville, Texas, on December 13, 1988. There was a hitch, because a tube attached to the needle in his arm began to leak, and it was necessary to make repairs before the execution could continue.

Legal Byways

Condemned criminals and their attorneys will do anything to cheat the executioner, and the record of seemingly endless appeals on various technicalities is exasperating. That this is even possible is evidence that the American system of criminal justice is extremely inefficient, and is barely capable of coping with even a fraction of the crimes committed. Perhaps the most ridiculous example of a pointless and fruitless delay came in 1980, when eight condemned prisoners brought suit against the Federal Food and Drug Administration regarding the unapproved use of drugs for executions. The case, eventually known as Chaney vs. Heckler, was finally defeated in March, 1985. It had gone up through several levels, and some of the language used was amusing. To request that the Food and Drug Administration pass judgment on whether a drug used for executions is "safe and effective" is absurd, but such is the state of our legal system today that this became part of the trial record.[10]

Execution by chemical injection leaves some people uneasy, even when it goes well. Margie Velma Barfield, a 52-year old grandmother, was executed in North Carolina on November 2, 1984 for the murder of her fiance in 1977. She had admitted to committing three other murders, and the one for which she was to die had been a poisoning. Thus, there was a certain irony to her death sentence. North Carolina was one of the states that had adopted lethal injection.

Barfield was the first female to die under any of the new capital punishment laws. Elizabeth Duncan had been gassed in California in 1962, before the moratorium on executions. An extra problem with Barfield's execution was that North Carolina's governor, James Hunt, was running for a Senate seat, and there were suspicions that his political enemies put him on the hot seat, trying to force him to make a clemency decision shortly before election day.[11] In any case, Barfield's execution was uneventful. She lay down on the gurney, and when the chemicals flowed into her vein, she closed her eyes, appeared to relax, and died quietly.

Doctors' Participation

Lethal injection has stimulated a sore point among doctors. Dr. Ruth Baine, of the Texas Medical Association, has voiced her opposition to doctors taking part in executions.[12] Now that lethal injection, which uses medical materials and techniques to kill, is a fact of American life, the argument has become acute.

A statement by the Judicial Council of the American Medical Association is a masterpiece of hypocrisy regarding the AMA's policy on doctors participating in executions. While recognizing that acceptance of capital punishment is a matter of individual conscience, it states that a physician "should not be a participant in a legally authorized execution," although it allows him to determine death afterwards.[13]

This statement ignores that the drugs used in legal executions are those recommended by doctors for their effects, and that doctors order them for the prison system. As they're all prescription drugs, only doctors can order them. Doctors also must train executioners on the technique of finding a vein and properly inserting a needle, so that the chemical execution may proceed efficiently.

Doctors have always taken part in executions. The guillotine was invented by one. Medical doctors played important roles in Nazi Germany's euthanasia program, as we've seen. In this country, they've always been part of legal executions. A doctor places a paper target over the heart in shooting executions. In an injection execution, the prisoner may have deeply-seated veins, and access to them may be beyond the ability of anyone without medical training. The accepted method of reaching a deep blood vessel is a "cut-down," done by a doctor.[14] In New Jersey, state law allows a doctor to sedate the condemned before the administration of the lethal drug. As we've seen, Montana law allows a doctor to perform the lethal injection.

The Anonymous Executioner

In previous eras, executioners were celebrities. Various hangmen became legends in their own times. Today, the executioner's identity is secret. In Utah, for example, the firing party is chosen and assembled in secret, and their identities are not released.[15] In other states, similar measures apply to keep the executioner's identity secret. In Washington state, a recent court decision served to confirm the state's right to keep the hangman's identity secret. Judge Daniel Berschauer, of Thurston County Superior Court, ruled against the American Civil Liberties Union, which had attempted to learn the name and qualifications of the hangman. This was an attempt to intimidate the executioner, who had stated that he would perform the execution of triple murderer Charles R. Campbell only if his identity remained secret. Campbell had stabbed two women and the 8-year-old daughter of one after his release from prison in 1982, as reprisal for one of the women testifying against him during a trial convicting him of rape in 1976.[16]

Keeping the executioner's identity secret is not very difficult. Restricting the information to few people, on a "need-to-know" basis, helps avoid leaks. A system of cash payment aids his anonymity.

This is the loophole through which doctors take part in executions without incurring the wrath of the American Medical Association or generating more negative publicity for an already heavily tarnished occupation. A medical doctor can, after the close of his office, drive down to a meeting place, such as a shopping center parking lot. A waiting van, driven by a prison officer, takes him to the prison, entering by a back gate out of sight of the press. In the execution chamber, he meets the prisoner, who is already strapped down on the gurney. A quick inspection tells him if he can simply insert the needle leading to the next room, or whether he must make a cut-down. If a cut-down is necessary, an injection of local anesthetic keeps the prisoner from feeling the pain of the scalpel. He attaches the leads from the electro-cardiograph to the prisoner's chest. The doctor retires to the special cubicle next door, where the tube from the prisoner's vein ends, attached to a bottle that steadily drips saline solution. He mixes the lethal cocktail in a syringe, and waits for his cue. The witnesses march into the execution chamber, but don't see the doctor because he's already behind the curtain.

When the signal comes from the warden, the doctor picks up his syringe and injects the solution into the tube, which rapidly conveys it into the prisoner's vein. After a couple of minutes, the beep-beep-beep of the EKG changes into a steady tone, and the prisoner is dead. After the witnesses leave, the doctor comes out, collects his envelope from the warden, and accompanies his driver to the van to begin the trip home.

Physician-Assisted Death

An increasing problem in the United States is that of old or terminally ill people who prefer to die instead of lingering. All states forbid mercy killing, by a doctor or anyone else. Whatever the motive, it's still murder under the law. Many states, additionally, prohibit assisting a suicide, and any doctor who provides a lethal drug dose for a patient is liable.

Michigan is one state that does not prohibit a physician from helping a patient's self-destruction. Dr. Jack Kevorkian, a retired pathologist, built a suicide machine to help people dispose of themselves humanely. The device is similar to those used for legal executions, and consists of a frame holding three bottles. One holds saline solution, another holds thiopental, and the third contains potassium chloride. A network of tubes and an electric motor injects the chemicals into the patient's vein in sequence. The saline comes first, to serve as a vehicle for the other chemicals and to show that the system is working properly. When the suicide pushes a button, the dose of thiopental produces unconsciousness, and a few seconds later the potassium chloride follows, to stop the heart.

The first person publicly revealed to have used the device was Janet Adkins, an Oregon woman with Alzheimer's Disease. She had to travel to Michigan because physician-assisted suicide is illegal in Oregon. The doctor, who stated that he did not charge for this service, drove her to a park, where he attached the tube to her vein. When Adkins pushed the button, the thiopental rendered her unconscious in 25 seconds, and the follow-up dose of potassium chloride caused death in five or six minutes.[17]

The doctor stated that he anticipated prosecution for this action, and that he considered using the device on himself one day.

Sources

1. *Capital Punishment and the American Agenda*, Franklin E. Zimring and Gordon Hawkins, New York, Cambridge University Press, 1986, p. 107.
2. *Ibid.*, p. 110.
3. *Capital Punishment*, Edited by Thomas Draper, New York, The H. W. Wilson Company, 1985, p. 149 and 156-157.
4. New Jersey State Statutes, #2C, 49-2.
5. Montana State Statutes, #49-19-103(3).
6. *Reviving The Death Penalty*, Gary E. McCuen and R. A. Baumgart, Hudson, WI, GEM Publications, 1985, p. 49.
7. *Capital Punishment*, p. 154.
8. *Executions*, George V. Bishop, Los Angeles, CA, Sherbourne Press, 1965, p. 37.
9. *Capital Punishment*, pp. 146-147.
10. *Capital Punishment and the American Agenda*, pp. 115-119.
11. *Ibid.*, pp. 126-128.

12. *Capital Punishment*, p. 155.
13. *Reviving The Death Penalty*, pp. 41-45.
14. *Capital Punishment*, p. 158.
15. *Executions*, George V. Bishop, p. 34.
16. Associated Press, May 5, 1990.
17. Associated Press, June 6, 1990.

13

Ceremonial Self-Execution

In certain cultures, and in certain occupations, the price of failure or dishonor is death. The Japanese military provide a good example. With the slogan: "Death is light as a feather and duty heavier than a mountain," they glorify death in battle. To a Japanese serviceman, failure to win in battle is dishonorable, unless he's killed in action. Surrender is unthinkable, the mark of cowardice.

Hara-kiri and Seppuku

Roughly translated, "hara-kiri" means suicide to defend one's honor, or to atone for misdeeds. "Seppuku" is the method of doing so, consisting of a self-inflicted stab into the abdomen, followed by an upward slash, and a transverse slash. This disembowelment is the traditional method of self-inflicted death among the Japanese.

This is a very difficult and painful method of dying, because although death is certain once the person has made the cuts, the process is slow, and death can take many minutes or even hours. This is why those who attempt this often engage another person to "assist" them. Once the person makes the initial cut, thereby proving his courage, the assistant traditionally beheads him. Beheading is going out of style, and shooting is now in vogue, especially among the military.

"Do The Right Thing"

In Europe, shooting has been the way out for a nobleman or military officer faced with dishonor. A notorious example was Colonel Alfred Redl, of the Austrian General Staff, before World War I. He had passed some of his country's most guarded secrets to the Russians for ten years, in return for payments which helped supplement his colonel's salary. Redl was a homosexual, in an era when there was no tolerance for homosexuality, especially among military officers, and this may have had something to do with his treason. It's unknown whether Redl found himself blackmailed by Russian agents, or whether he sold his country's secrets simply for money, which he used to support his lifestyle and possibly buy the services of male prostitutes.

In March, 1913, the Austrian counter-espionage agency intercepted two envelopes addressed to a pseudonym care of general delivery in Vienna. One contained 6,000 crowns in money and the other 8,000.[1] This was a lot of money for those days, and the method of delivery reeked of something clandestine. Austrian detectives staked out the post office, and followed the person who called for the mail. They reported back to Major Ronge, the counter-espionage chief, that the recipient of the envelopes was Colonel Redl. Major Ronge, in turn, reported this to the Austrian High Command and then the ship hit the sand. A detail of officers visited Colonel Redl, and questioned him about his activities. He replied that the evidence would be found in his house in Prague, and requested that one of them leave him a pistol. One of the officers lent him his, as this was an era when the word of a gentleman was just that, and nobody feared that Redl would use the handgun to shoot his way out. The tacit understanding was that he would do the gentlemanly thing and kill himself, which he did. When they returned, several hours later, they found Redl with a suicide note.

Self-destruction often saves the state the cost of a trial. However, there's no reason to suppose that self-execution will become a popular course of action. Criminals almost always wait for someone else to put an end to their lives, and there will always be work for executioners. Let's examine what the future might bring.

Sources

1. *Cry Spy!*, Burke Wilkinson, Englewood Cliffs, NJ, Bradbury Press, 1969, p. 8.

14

The Future of Executions

There's no reason to think that execution will ever go out of style, and there are several good reasons to foresee an increase in the number of executions. World population growth may well result in the view that life is cheap, and human life especially so. Population control will probably lead to an increase in abortions, and if the lives of the innocent are forfeit to control population, what value can the lives of criminals have?

Even in an extreme case of nuclear war, chances are that survivors, if any, will still execute criminals. If only a few hundred survivors are left, each life will be precious, but this won't necessarily preclude executions. Society simply won't be able to afford assigning a guard detail to run a prison, and anyone sentenced to life imprisonment would be a drain on precious resourccs.

Islamic Executions

The resurgence of Islam probably means more executions. The Islamic religion is strong on capital punishment, even for acts that we in the West would not consider criminal. The death sentence (without trial) passed upon Salman Rushdie, author of *The Satanic Verses*, is an example of what Islam holds for the blasphemer. Other crimes offending against the Koran have their own penalties, and most Moslem countries have capital punishment.

The Developing Countries

Most nations have capital punishment during the early stages of their development. Some feel that, as a society matures, the need for executions recedes, citing as proof the almost complete abolition of executions in Western Europe. This is still an open question, because we have yet to see if the increases in both crime and terrorist violence will cause European countries to reverse their policies.

What is certain, however, is that practically all African and Asian countries have capital punishment. In both Africa and Asia, there are Moslem and non-Moslem countries. Moslem countries tend to abide by traditional methods of execution, as followed for many centuries. Non-Moslem countries tend to choose more modern methods, following the Western pattern of making executions as quick as possible. The rope and the firing squad are common choices.

Advances in Execution Technology

Execution technology may change drastically in coming years. Execution by laser is a theoretical possibility.[1] Strapping the prisoner into a chair would be the first step, as in preparing for a firing squad execution. Upon a signal from the warden, the executioner would turn on the laser, which would drill a hot hole through the prisoner's head, frying his brain instantly.

A novel method, using off-the-shelf technology, is the "zapper box." This is a microwave oven with the door removed and the safety shorted. This allows operating the unit without the door in place. Strapping the prisoner tightly to a board allows inserting his head into the microwave oven's cavity. For safety, guards and witnesses would have to be in the next room before the executioner turned on the microwave oven with a remote switch. It might be worthwhile to anesthetize the prisoner, for his comfort and to reduce struggling. A fighting prisoner might wrench his head out of the oven before the execution was complete.

Depending on the wattage, it would take between one and ten minutes before the prisoner lost consciousness, as his brain slowly cooked. Death would take place when his brain activity stopped, in a few more minutes. A stethoscope would be a convenient way of ascertaining the moment.

Another method, again using electricity, is adapting an electric anesthesia or electro-shock machine for lethal applications. In electro-shock therapy, a jolt of between 80 and 150 volts of alternating current runs between two electrodes placed on the temples, for about one second. When the current hits, breathing stops, to resume about 30 seconds later. Voltages and techniques vary. The trend today is to apply the current to only one side of the brain, and to use lower voltage. Formerly, the "glissando" technique was in vogue, with a timer and rheostat starting the current at about 70 volts, and sliding up the scale to 120 or 150 volts in about one second. Advocates claimed that produced more convulsions for less current.

Electrical anesthesia requires an electrode on the front of the skull, and one at the rear. Alternating current of at least 70 volts is necessary to produce unconsciousness. The machine has a rheostat to vary the voltage, and the current stays on as long as the operator wishes. A simple on/off switch controls the duration.

A similar device was in use among some psychiatrists three decades ago. This small machine sold under the trade name of "SED-AC," and was very compact, for use in home treatments. Recommended use was to sedate a patient with electricity through the brain before applying a full electro-shock, but it was also useful for instant sedation in other cases, such as extreme anxiety attacks or psychotic episodes. This device never gained great popularity because the effect faded as soon as the operator turned off the current.

Adapting these for executions requires only rewiring to allow application of enough voltage to stop breathing. An on/off switch is necessary, because to ensure death, respiration must stop for several minutes. The execution procedure would require strapping the condemned person to a hospital gurney or a table, moistening the temples with conductive jelly, applying the electrodes, and switching on the current. In some electro-shock machines, the electrodes are mounted on insulated tongs, because they have to be in place for only a few seconds. Some accessory sets, however, have electrode plates mounted on a plastic or rubber headband which attaches with snaps or Velcro. This is more practical for executions, because the electrodes must remain in place for several minutes.

A mini-electrocution would be simpler to run than the traditional electric chair, which is expensive and uses a large amount of current. Because the brain is truly the most vulnerable organ to destroy in an execution, a future method may be an electric version of the pistol shot to the brain. Placing an electrode on each temple would allow the use of house current to render the prisoner unconscious and cook the brain, leaving the rest of the body relatively cool and unharmed. This method would be as painless as conventional electro-shock treatments. Using straps to restrain the prisoner would avoid any problems with convulsions. These probably would not occur anyway, because the current would remain on until the brain was destroyed.

Chemical Sedation

A serious problem for any executioner or death row officer is the condemned prisoner who fights. Although some punks make a show of bravado in court, and during the months or years while their appeals are following their course through the legal maze, when the final hours come they lose their nerve. Some are trembling wrecks when the guards come to escort them down the corridor, but others become belligerent. They can be extremely dangerous because they truly have nothing to lose, and many prison officials feel that it's not worth risking a guard's life or health if there are means to incapacitate them before the execution.

One way to control an unruly prisoner, as we've seen, is a harsh and thorough beating. A more modern way is an aerosol product called "CAP-STUN II." Another way is the administration of a powerful tranquilizer several hours before the execution. One is phenylephrine, under the brand name of "Phenergan." This drug, in a 50-mg. dose, tranquilizes the subject. 100 mgs. will put him into a daze, and he won't be able to resist being walked or carried to the execution chamber.

It's already common for the prison doctor to visit the prisoner before the execution, to give him a last examination to certify that he's "fit" for execution. At that time, he may ask the prisoner if he wants a sedative. If the prisoner consents, the doctor can administer whichever sedative he prefers, or has found most effective under the circumstances.

Without consent, it's still possible to mash the pills and mix them with food or drink. It's best if sedation begins at least 24 hours before the execution, which makes it easier to administer drugs with the food.

If the prisoner is totally wild and unruly, and won't eat, it's still possible to control him with CAP-STUN and administer drugs by injection. Once the first tranquilizer "takes," it will be easier to administer additional doses. Starting with Phenergan, it's possible to keep the prisoner under the effects of a "chemical lobotomy" until his execution.

Electronic Prisoner Control

Among the well-known and well-documented side-effects of electro-shock therapy are confusion and disorientation. This suggests a method of ensuring the docility of condemned prisoners on death row. During the last few days preceding the execution, administering a short series of electro-shock treatments each day would keep the prisoner dazed, and unable to resist. Often, one treatment per day is enough to dissolve short-term memory, and produce a confusional state. Applying two or three would guarantee results, and make it much easier for the death row crew to transport the prisoner to the execution chamber. A bonus effect would be that it would make the last days of confinement more humane, as the prisoner would probably be too disoriented to realize that his execution was imminent.

An off-the-shelf method of subject control is the "stun gun," or electronic zapper. These are available for less than one hundred dollars for top-of-the-line units. A stun gun acts through pain and shock, very much like a kick to the testicles. Most people react by going limp and falling to the floor, and become very docile. Recommended use is to apply about five seconds' shock to the torso, but in the case of a condemned prisoner, applying the electrodes to the neck would have a quicker effect, producing collapse.

Off-the-shelf Anesthesia

Because the trend in executions has been towards using simpler methods, and avoiding pain for the condemned, another possible method is using non-lethal gas and excluding oxygen. Nitrous oxide and carbon dioxide are well-suited for executions. Nitrous oxide is an anesthetic, and inhaling 100% gas produces unconsciousness within a minute, at most. Carbon dioxide also has toxic properties, and 100% administration produces quick loss of consciousness.

The prisoner would have to be strapped down, because this method requires using an ordinary anesthesia mask over the face. A tank of pure nitrous oxide or pure carbon dioxide would serve as the anesthetic. Within a minute of administering pure gas, the prisoner becomes unconscious. Without oxygen mixed with the anesthetic gas, the prisoner would be oxygen-starved and brain-dead within four or five minutes. The appeal of this method is that it can work with anyone, without any need to find a vein, and without requiring a doctor to administer the anesthetic. An additional point, for favorable public relations, is that administration of the gas causes no pain at all, not even the prick of a needle.

A significant advantage of this method is that there is no danger to personnel involved in the execution. Cyanide gas requires decontamination before guards can enter the death chamber to remove the body. An exhaust fan must run for several minutes to vent the hydrogen cyanide into the outside atmosphere. An ammonia spray is necessary to neutralize any remaining gas. The prisoner must dress lightly, to avoid pockets of lethal gas in the clothing. Using nitrous oxide or carbon dioxide, with a face mask, would eliminate all of these problems.

Gas anesthesia is also useful for supplementing conventional executions. Administering anesthetic gas to a prisoner strapped in the electric chair is one merciful way of eliminating pain. Administering it in his cell, while he's lying on his bunk, would spare him the final moments of anxiety while walking the "last mile" and being strapped into the chair.

Although it's fairly certain that a bullet in the back of the head is painless, rendering the prisoner unconscious would make sure. It would make it easier for the executioner by keeping the prisoner from moving during the last critical seconds, and possibly spoiling his aim.

Another off-the-shelf technique is electro-shock anesthesia. In the heyday of prefrontal lobotomies, one technique was to blast the patient into unconsciousness with an application of electro-shock, then insert the leucotome under his eyelids into the brain before he awakened. This worked because trans-orbital lobotomy was very quick. It took only a few seconds to lift the eyelid, insert the icepick-like leucotome under it aimed at the brain, tap it through the thin bone of the orbital cavity, and swing it in a 60-degree arc. A skilled lobotomist could do both sides on a patient while he was still unconscious.

Although there is no documented case of this application in executions, performing a lobotomy upon a condemned prisoner during the hours before his execution is one way of making him tractable. The technique of transorbital lobotomy is so simple that even a prison doctor should have no problem with it. The prisoner would be so dazed from the effects of the lobotomy that he would be only dimly aware of what was happening.

The only objection would be from traditionalists, who feel that an important part of the death penalty is that the condemned person be awake and aware of what's happening. In this light, executing an unconscious or unknowing subject is useless, because the entire point of the penalty is lost.

Scavenging

Organ transplant technology has created a demand for human organs far beyond what current sources can supply. This brings the prospect of obtaining fresh human organs from condemned prisoners who otherwise would undergo conventional execution. A conventional execution is often wasteful, in the sense that many vital and healthy organs are totally destroyed, and made useless for transplants. Electrocution cooks the entire body, leaving nothing for salvage. Conventional firing squads fire into the chest cavity, and marksmanship is often so poor that bullets destroy the lungs, liver, spleen, and other organs, as well as the heart.

The main advantage of using condemned prisoners as living organ banks is that most murderers are young. Unless they're seriously ill with an incurable disease, or have other medical disqualifications, their youth works in favor of obtaining organs in top condition.

It would probably require a Constitutional amendment in the United States, but a person sentenced to death would be a good source of spare parts. This might be by informed consent or by decision of the court. The procedure would probably be as follows:

A medical examination would determine the prisoner's general condition and which organs were suitable for transplant. A badly deteriorated body, such as that of an old prisoner, or one totally ravaged by drugs, would not be a good choice. There would also have to be serological tests, to ensure that the person was not infected with hepatitis or AIDS.

Using informed consent mode, a doctor would explain the choices to the prisoner. The prisoner could do nothing, and the sentence would be conventional execution by whichever method was legal in that state. The alternative would be to sign a consent form, and allow a team of transplant surgeons to remove all needed organs. The prisoner would experience little discomfort, because the surgery would take place in a conventional operating room, with general anesthesia, the difference being that the prisoner would not wake up.

Mandated organ stripping would work the same way, but regardless of the condemned prisoner's consent. It would require the same degree of coordination as conventional transplants, with recipients present in adjoining operating rooms to receive the organs as the main surgical team removed them.

Under both plans, the prisoner would receive excellent care during the weeks before the transplanting session, as it would be important to keep him in top physical condition. Except for the involuntary confinement, he would enjoy V.I.P. status, with tasty and well-prepared food, enough entertainment to keep him in good spirits, and the best medical care.

In some cases, however, the psychological pressure of impending dissection would be too much to bear, and it might become necessary to use drugs to keep the prisoner sedated. An alternative, realistic because the prisoner's brain would be expendable, would be to perform a radical prefrontal lobotomy on all prisoners entering this program. Modern technology, using electrodes inserted under the eyelids and driven into the brain, permits selective ablation of brain tissue with minimal operative risk. A thorough lobotomy, with extensive destruction of frontal lobe tissue, would ensure that the prisoner would be dazed and disoriented regarding his eventual fate. An alternative method of selective destruction of brain tissue is the injection of phenol. This is quick and low-tech, requiring only insertion of the appropriate needle through the orbital cavity.

The only objection to transplanting organs from condemned prisoners might be an esthetic one. Some potential recipients might feel uncomfortable at receiving a murderer's heart or lungs, for example. Such persons would, of course, have the choice of waiting for transplants to become available through conventional channels. There would probably be a long enough waiting list for condemned prisoners' organs to ensure that none would go to waste. Another method would be to offer transplants anonymously, without the recipient knowing their source.

While it might be wrong to call execution a growth industry, it's certain that state-sanctioned death is not going out of style. In the United States, as well as most other countries in the world, executions will continue for many years to come.

Sources

1. *Capital Punishment and the American Agenda*, Franklin E. Zimring and Gordon Hawkins, New York, Cambridge University Press, 1986, p. 123.

Index

Adkins, Janet, 96
American Medical Association, 32, 88, 93
Anesthesia, 80, 87, 90, 95, 105, 109, 110, 112
Argentine Method, 35
Asphyxia, 69
Athenians, 6
Auto-da-fe, 11
Autry J. D., 91

Baine Dr. Ruth, 93
Barbiturate, 90
Barfield, Margie Velma, 92, 93
Beheading, 6, 38, 42, 43, 44, 45, 46, 48, 60, 100
Berschauer, Judge Daniel, 94
Blindfold, 32, 66
Block, Eugene B., 21
Brooks Charlie, 89, 90, 91
Burning at the stake, 9, 10, 11, 53
Byrne, Edward R., 21

Calcraft, William, 34
California Supreme Court, 71
Campbell, Charles R., 95

Canaris, Admiral Wilhelm, 41, 52
Cap-Stun, 32, 107, 108
Capital punishment, 2, 3, 6, 7, 10, 12, 13, 14, 15, 19, 20, 21, 24, 37, 45, 48, 61, 88, 89, 91, 93, 104
Carbon dioxide, 109, 110
Ceremonial killing, 1, 11, 99
Chaney vs. Heckler, 92
Chemical lobotomy, 108
Chemical sedation, 107
Chessman, Caryl, 24, 70, 71
Chloroform, 75
Choking to death, 39
Convulsions, 23, 24, 69, 78, 79, 80, 89, 105, 107
Corporal punishment, 5
Coup de grace, 33, 58, 59
Court-martial, 34, 56, 58, 62
Crime rates, 13
Crucifixion, 9, 10
Curare, 90
Cyanide gas, 69, 89, 110

Death machine, 23
Death of a Thousand Cuts, 52
Death squads, 35
Death warrant, 27
Death watch, 28
Decapitation, 39, 45, 73
Deterrence, 13, 28, 34
Disemboweling, 10, 11
Disembowelment, 100
Doctors, 2, 32, 33, 46, 75, 87, 90, 93, 94, 95
Drawing and quartering, 2, 10, 11, 46, 49
Drop chart, 39, 40
Duke of Rothingham, 44

Effects of electrocution, 23
Einsatzgruppen, 62
Electric chair, 2, 21, 23, 32, 55, 60, 76, 78, 82, 83, 89, 106, 110
Electrical anesthesia, 106
Electro-shock therapy, 71, 79, 80, 105, 106, 107, 108, 110
Electrocution, 15, 21, 22, 32, 72, 73, 74, 75, 77, 78, 79, 80, 81, 82, 83, 84, 87, 88, 89, 111
Electrodes, 23, 74, 76, 79, 105, 106, 107, 109, 113
Electronic Prisoner Control, 108
Entombment, 52
Escort detail, 31, 57, 77, 107
Execution by laser, 104
Execution of children, 11
Executioner, 11, 22, 24, 38, 41, 43, 44, 45, 46, 47, 49, 50, 51, 52, 53, 56, 74, 75, 76, 78, 82, 91, 92, 94, 105, 107, 110

Experiments, 46, 48

Field-expedient methods, 61
Final visits, 30
Firing squad, 6, 15, 32, 33, 34, 45, 55, 56, 57, 58, 59, 60, 61, 62, 83, 104, 105, 111
Florida State Prison, 83
Francis, Willie, 82, 83

Gallows, 40
Garrote, 51, 52
Garroting, 38
Gas chamber, 2, 24, 67, 68, 69, 70, 71, 84, 89
Genickschuss, 56
Gilmore, Gary, 15, 20, 61
Goering, Hermann, 28, 41
Graham, Barbara, 24
Graunger, Thomas, 1
Gray, Jimmy Lee, 69
Guillotin, Dr. Joseph Ignace, 46
Guillotine, 2, 33, 46, 47, 48, 94

Hale, Nathan, 41
Handcuffs, 31
Hanging, 10, 11, 15, 28, 35, 37, 38, 39, 40, 41, 42, 45, 61, 73
Hara-kiri, 99
Hemlock, poison, 9
Hitler, Adolf, 41, 52
Holding cell, 77

Iron Maiden, 11
Islamic Executions, 104

Jesus Christ, 10
Joan of Arc, 10
Jodl, Field Marshal Alfred, 41
Juveniles, 42, 85

Kaltenbrunner, S.S. General Ernst, 41
Keitel, Field Marshal Wilhelm, 41
Kemmler, William, 74, 75
Ketch, Jack, 37, 38
Kevorkian, Dr. Jack, 96
Koestler, Arthur, 22

Landry, Raymond, 92
Last cigarette, 29
Last drink, 29, 30
Last letters, 30
Last meal, 29
Last mile, 23, 31, 110
Last statement, 31
Lethal injection, 15, 55, 84, 87, 88, 89, 93, 94
Living organ banks, 111, 112
Lobotomy, 110, 111, 113
Lody, 66
Lody, Carl Hans, 60

Loeb, Robert, 20
Lord Lovat, 44
Lord Russell, 38

Mass executions, 63, 64
Mass media, 19
McCracken, Henry, 71
McLendon, James, 22
Microwave oven, 105
Mini-electrocution, 106
Morphine, 75, 90
Murder rate, 16, 20
Mutilation, 5

Nitrous oxide, 109, 110
Nuremburg Trials, 41

Organ transplants, 106, 111, 112
Orwell, George, 22

Painless execution, 14, 53, 107
Par-boiling, 53
Pavulon, 80, 90
Peine Forte et Dure, 50
Pelletier, Nicolas-Jacques, 47
Penitentiary, 5, 81
Phenergan, 107, 108
Phenol, 87
Phenylephrine, 107
Physician, 90, 93
Physician-assisted death, 96
Piano wire, 41, 42
Pierce, Robert, 71
Poisoning, 92
Potassium chloride, 90, 97
Potassium cyanide, 68

Red-hot irons, 14
Redl, Colonel Alfred, 100, 101
Religious Counsel, 30
Rosenberg, Julius and Ethel, 80, 81, 82

Sacco, Nicola, 83
Sadistic sexual perversion, 50
Sedation, 33, 90, 94, 106, 108, 113
Self-destruction, 101
Slovik, Private Eddie, 58, 59, 60, 66
Snyder, Ruth, 78
Socrates, 9, 10
Spanish Inquisition, 11, 50
Spenkelink, John, 76
Stephens, Alpha Otis, 76
Stinney, George, 82
Strangulation, 38, 41, 42, 52, 73
Stroop, 72
Stroop, S.S. General Jurgen, 41
Stun gun, 32, 109
Submental knot, 39
Suicide, 28, 99, 101
Suicide machine, 96
Sulfuric acid, 68

Supreme Court, 14, 15, 61, 88, 89

Tafero, Joseph, 83, 84
Taylor, William, 75
Thiopental, 90, 97
Third Reich, 87
Thorpe, Roderick, 22
Thuggees, 51
Torture, 11, 13, 42, 51, 53
Traitors, 6, 60
Tranquilizer, 107, 108
Treason, 6, 100

Vanzetti, Bartomlomeo, 83
Victims' rights, 3, 19
Vigilantes, 37

Witnesses, 28, 29, 31, 32, 34, 60, 67, 75, 76, 77, 78, 95, 96, 105
Women, 10, 11, 51, 63, 70